Reconnecting
Disadvantaged
Young Men

Peter Edelman
Harry J. Holzer
Paul Offner

Reconnecting Disadvantaged Young Men

URBAN INSTITUTE PRESS
Washington, D.C.

Library of Congress Cataloging-in-Publication Data

Edelman, Peter B.
   Reconnecting disadvantaged young men / Peter Edelman, Harry J. Holzer, Paul Offner.
      p. cm.
   Includes bibliographical references and index.
   ISBN 0-87766-728-4 (pbk. : alk. paper)
   1. Young men—United States. 2. African American youth.
   3. Youth—Services for—United States. 4. Youth—Government policy
   —United States.   I. Holzer, Harry J., 1957-   . II. Offner, Paul.
   III. Title.
   HQ799.6.E34 2005
   362.508421'0973—dc22

2005032875

ISBN 0-87766-728-4 (paper, alk. paper)

Printed in the United States of America

10 09 08 07 06 05   1 2 3 4 5

THE URBAN INSTITUTE is a nonprofit, nonpartisan policy research and educational organization established in Washington, D.C., in 1968. Its staff investigates the social, economic, and governance problems confronting the nation and evaluates the public and private means to alleviate them. The Institute disseminates its research findings through publications, its Web site, the media, seminars, and forums.

Through work that ranges from broad conceptual studies to administrative and technical assistance, Institute researchers contribute to the stock of knowledge available to guide decisionmaking in the public interest.

Conclusions or opinions expressed in Institute publications are those of the authors and do not necessarily reflect the views of officers or trustees of the Institute, advisory groups, or any organizations that provide financial support to the Institute.

*Our colleague and coauthor
Paul Offner passed away on
April 20, 2004. Before he became ill,
he contributed enormously to this volume.
We dedicate it to his memory.*

Contents

Acknowledgments ix

Foreword xi

1 Reconnecting Disadvantaged Young Men
   An Introduction 1

2 The Characteristics of Disconnected Young Men
   A Review of Evidence, Literature, and Context 11

3 Education and Training Policies 37

4 Building Community Youth Systems 67

5 Improving Financial Incentives for
   Low-Wage Work 79

6 Reconnecting Noncustodial Parents
   and Ex-Offenders 99

7 Summary and Conclusion 123

References 133

About the Authors 145

Index 147

Acknowledgments

W e are grateful to the Hewlett Foundation for their financial support, and especially to Michael Wald for his comments and support throughout the writing of the report that ultimately became the manuscript for this book. We have benefited from outstanding research assistance from Tim Dore, Jennifer Rikoski, and Emily Rosenberg, for which we are grateful as well. Adam Carasso and Elaine Sorensen also helped us simulate the costs and effects of our various proposals to expand the earned income tax credit. We benefited greatly from discussions with Gordon Berlin, Doug Besharov, Betsy Brand, David Brown, Len Burman, Erik Butler, Geoffrey Canada, David Ellwood, Ron Ferguson, Sundra Franklin, Linda Harris, James Head, Janet Holtzblatt, Rob Ivry, Richard Kazis, David Lah, Bob Lerman, Jeffrey Liebman, Hilary Pennington, Hugh Price, Wendell Primus, Sally Prouty, Karen Sitnick, Elaine Sorensen, William Spring, Gene Steuerle, Dorothy Stoneman, Jeremy Travis, Vicki Turetsky, Ray Uhalde, Gary Walker, and Joan Wynn. Rob Ivry, Jeffrey Liebman, and Wendell Primus also gave us comments on early chapter drafts. Two anonymous referees also provided very helpful comments on the entire draft. All remaining errors are our own.

Foreword

Peter Edelman, a distinguished professor at Georgetown University Law Center, this spring asked me to write a foreword for a new book he had coauthored with Harry Holzer of the Georgetown Public Policy Institute and the late Paul Offner of the Urban Institute. I consented on the spot because Peter is a longstanding friend and professional role model and because I greatly admire his collaborators. Whatever they thought worth writing would be worth heralding to wider audiences.

Then I spotted the title—*Reconnecting Disadvantaged Young Men.* Instantly I knew, without cracking a page of their book, that it would be thought provoking and important. I've devoted much of my professional career to trying to create programs and advance public policies that reopen the mainstream to young people who've dropped out of school, the labor force, and life. Having now read the book, it more than lives up to its advance billing. Mr. Edelman, Mr. Holzer, and Mr. Offner have done the country an enormous service by thrusting the plight—and the potential—of anonymous young men back onto society's radar screen.

As I read *Reconnecting Disadvantaged Young Men,* one particularly poignant comment in the text kept recurring. "Young black men," noted the authors, "are the least popular group in America with politicians." Perversely enough, the only potent lobby that looks after their food, clothing, and shelter is the prison-industrial complex, which thrives on incarcerating them. I know from firsthand experience as an erstwhile legal services lawyer, mentor, and former CEO of the National Urban League, that many aimless young men would hardly qualify as angels. Far from it.

Yet this dire situation needn't be so. With its incisive research, astute analysis, and compelling policy prescriptions, *Reconnecting Disadvantaged Young Men* points the way to a brighter future for these young men, their families and dependents, and the communities they inhabit. They aren't lost causes by any stretch of the imagination.

Disconnection isn't a new phenomenon among young men. Nearly a half century ago, sociologists were writing about anomie among teenagers. The persistence of juvenile delinquency among urban youth provided much of the impetus for the War on Poverty in the 1960s. In the 1970s, compassionate economists agonized about the dual labor market that seemed to lock young black men into alarmingly high rates of structural unemployment.

So we've seen this picture before. But today it seems bleaker and the problems more intractable. Explanations abound about why millions of young men, a dismayingly high proportion of whom are black and Latino, are stranded in a state of disconnection. The authors quite patiently walk us through several theories, most of which ring true to me, especially these: The urban-based manufacturing economy has virtually collapsed, destroying good-paying jobs and decent lifestyles for marginally skilled male workers. Public schools have lagged shamelessly behind in equipping urban youngsters to meet the stiffer intellectual and skill demands of working in the knowledge economy. And robust immigration has brought an influx of workers willing to work for the minimum wage or, often, less.

Well-documented discrimination by employers places African-American job applicants at a decided disadvantage. And, make no mistake, Jim Crow still lives inside the criminal justice system, with its disparate treatment of black and Latino males every step of the way, from apprehension and arrest to sentencing to incarceration. That said, the disturbingly high rate of criminality among disconnected youth renders them virtually unemployable, which reinforces their economic and social isolation. Another little-noticed explanation is the disinclination of the U.S. military to accept high school dropouts, thus closing an exit from poverty and aimlessness that inner-city fellows relied on when I was growing up in the 1950s. Finally, at the admitted risk of blaming the victim, disaffected males who embrace "gangsta" speech, affect, and attire seal their disconnection from the American mainstream.

So much for the disheartening diagnosis. What's refreshing about *Reconnecting Disadvantaged Young Men* is Mr. Edelman, Mr. Holzer, and Mr. Offner's highly pragmatic policy recommendations for getting these young men back on a positive track. Just as the diagnoses range far and wide, so could the policy prescriptions. Yet the authors, rather than proselytize for every policy that would help, focus on three key policy areas, namely

- enhancing education, training, and employment opportunities for disadvantaged youth;
- improving the incentives of less-skilled young workers—particularly low-income men—to accept employment; and
- addressing particularly severe barriers and disincentives faced by some youth, such as ex-offenders and noncustodial fathers.

The prescriptive sections of the book should inspire us anew to muster the political will to invest in disadvantaged young men. As the authors make abundantly clear, much can be done to make a difference in the lives of these young men, in their families, and in their communities.

Reflecting back on my own professional career, I can attest that disconnected young men aren't lost causes to be consigned to the people dumpsters we call prisons. When I was in law school in the mid-1960s, I earned extra money by working for the local antipoverty agency as a social group worker. My group consisted of a half-dozen junior high school boys who were constantly in and out of the clutches of juvenile court. The idea behind hiring me was to link the kids with a caring adult who might be able to get them back on the right track before they went totally off the rails.

We hung out together and talked about everything and nothing. We shot hoops and even formed a basketball team that competed in the park recreation league. That was important because it introduced structure and teamwork into their aimless lives. I'd take them to New York City to see the sights and ride on the Staten Island ferry. They visited our apartment, where we baked cakes. I dropped by their homes to get to know their families, usually a mother or grandmother and several siblings, but seldom a father in sight.

During the two years we were together, these fellows had nary another encounter with the cops. They stayed completely out of trouble and pushed on through school, although admittedly it was a struggle. We really connected, and some of the guidance and support I had hoped to provide actually penetrated.

I didn't realize how much our relationship had come to mean to them until I showed up late one day because a law school class had run over the allotted time. One of the youngsters, speaking on behalf of his buddies, told me something that has stuck with me ever since. "Mr. Price," he began, "being together with you and the guys at three o'clock has become the most important thing in our lives. If we're going to keep this going, we need to know that being here at three o'clock is also the most important thing in your life," he continued. "If you're ever late again, we'll know it isn't and that'll be it for us."

In other words, I gained an early understanding of the wisdom of one of the key policy prescriptions advanced in this book: creating community-based systems that support the academic and social development of young males on the brink of disconnection from school.

Fast forward two decades to another telling lesson. The support system in this instance is rooted in a starkly different community, namely the U.S. military. Here, too, the authors acknowledge the potential of military models by citing the National Guard Youth ChalleNGe Corps as a promising approach for getting the lives of disconnected youth back on track.

I agree wholeheartedly with the authors, because the results appear to bear their optimism. And, to be upfront about it, because I'm one of the parents who helped conceive the Youth ChalleNGe Corps.

When I was growing up in the 1950s, many of my classmates simply weren't into school. Try as the teachers might, they just couldn't turn these youngsters on to learning. Some were cut-ups and truants. A few of the boys were what we quaintly called "roughnecks" who barely escaped reform school. Others probably possessed the array of nonacademic "intelligences," written about by Howard Gardner of Harvard, that make traditional schools an unbearable bore for some young people.

As soon as they could, some of my disaffected classmates would drop out of school and out of sight. I recall encountering them years later. Somehow they had managed to enlist in the Army—or else they'd been drafted. Either way, they strutted about proudly in their uniforms, with a discernible sense of purpose. The Army had turned them around by successfully instilling a basic lesson of military life: if you do a job well, you get ahead.

Years ago, the Army worked wonders with aimless young men. What's the explanation? Beyond the armed forces' legendary discipline, my strong hunch is that the intricate system of ranks and incentives helped motivate young people who cannot see far over the horizon.

Unfortunately, the military eventually went upscale and stopped accepting school dropouts. This shut off an important escape route and road to salvation for desperate inner-city and rural youngsters with nowhere else to turn, costing society—and successive generations of these young people—dearly.

Barely weeks after becoming vice president of the Rockefeller Foundation in 1988, I attended an Accelerated Schools conference at the Stanford University School of Education. There I heard my friend and mentor, Edmond Gordon of Yale, say that he feared the condition of urban youngsters was so grim that it might be time to "conscript them for their own good."

His provocative observation sparked an idea that had long been germinating in my mind. In the spring of 1989, I asked the National Guard to create a residential youth corps for teenagers who had dropped out of school. General Herb Temple, the national commander of the Guard, and Dan Donohue, the Guard's director of public information—much to my astonishment—embraced the idea with great enthusiasm and minimal persuasion, and pledged to work on making it happen.

At the same time, I got the Foundation to make grants to the Center for Strategic and International Studies (CSIS), a defense policy think tank, and to Public/Private Ventures (P/PV), a research outfit focused on mentoring programs for young people. The idea of the grants was for these organizations, highly regarded in their respective fields, to conduct a feasibility study of the concept of a quasi-military corps for dropouts. General Temple and Dan Donohue said feasibility studies were fine. But they intended to forge ahead with mobilizing the National Guard, including rounding up the pilot funding from Congress. Nevertheless, working with P/PV, CSIS established a study group known as the National Community Service for Out-of-School Youth Project, which was cochaired by Senator John McCain and Representative Dave McCurdy.

All of this collective energy spawned what came to be known as the National Guard Youth ChalleNGe Corps. In 1993, it opened for business in 10 states. The program design called for participants, all of whom must be school dropouts, to spend five months on a military base. Participants received academic instruction and leadership training, along with tips on preparing a resume. Equally important, youth also are taught "follower-ship" skills, namely how to be a team player and take orders from super-visors without taking offense. In addition, the participants are paired with National Guard mentors who stick with them for a year once they graduate, helping them apply to college and land jobs.

The first contingent of ChalleNGe Corps kids in the nation graduated from Connecticut's Camp Ella Grasso in 1993. Young people who six months earlier had been written off as borderline worthless strode down the aisle proudly decked out in caps and gowns. An audience of nearly 1,000 parents, grandparents, children, and other well-wishers cheered them on. Some grizzled American Legion veterans bestowed the Legion's traditional "top student" honor of one of the graduates. A chorus made up of participants who first met at the camp sang several tunes, surprisingly well at that.

The National Guard Youth Foundation web site (http://www.ngyouth foundation.org) contains up-to-date information on the ChalleNGe Corps. These days, the program serves upwards of 5,000 16- to 18-year-olds in 25 states and Puerto Rico, with additional states in queue to start units. Youth ChalleNGe Corps's retention rate of roughly 90 percent is impressive enough. Nearly 53,000 young people have graduated since its inception in 1993. Over 73 percent have completed the requirements for their GEDs or high school diplomas. Evidently, that's 12 percent higher than the national rate. Seventy percent of the corps members have landed jobs, enrolled in continuing education, or joined the military within 30 days of graduation. And per-participant costs run roughly one-fifth of the cost of incarceration. Corporate executives would envy this rate of return on investment.

Wary of terrorism, fearful of economic insecurity, and absorbed in our own lives, we Americans suffer today from a collective case of social conscience deficit disorder. Thanks to tax cuts favoring the wealthiest among us, the federal government professes to be broke when it comes to mounting new domestic initiatives that cost real money.

By proposing bold interventions for fellow citizens who aren't the least bit popular with politicians, the authors of *Reconnecting Disadvantaged Young Men* have embarked on an arduous journey of policymaking and moral suasion. I salute them for their distinctive blend of compassion and pragmatism, because the journey must begin somewhere and sometime. And it must begin now before another generation of disadvantaged young men perishes spiritually and economically.

What a waste it is to write off disconnected young people. Consider the staggering cost to society of maintaining prisons, welfare, and foster care. According to the U.S. Census Bureau, the average cost in lost productivity and wages for each high school dropout may total as much as $900,000. Think of the taxes the dropouts would have paid into the government's coffers and the fair share of baby boomers' Social Security benefits they could have borne.

Several years ago, I heard a guest on the PBS *Newshour with Jim Lehrer* say that for World War II veterans from poor and working class families, the G. I. Bill was their magic carpet to the American mainstream. The enlightened investments proposed in *Reconnecting Disadvantaged Young Men* could become the 21st century magic carpet for hundreds of thousands of disadvantaged young men who fear they'll never get another shot at the American Dream.

Hugh Price
Senior Advisor
DLA Piper Rudnick Gray Cary US LLP

1

Reconnecting Disadvantaged Young Men

An Introduction

By several recent counts, the United States is home to 2 to 3 million youth age 16 through 24 who are without postsecondary education and "disconnected" from the worlds of school and work (Wald and Martinez 2003). By "disconnected," we mean young people who are not in school and have been out of work for a substantial period, roughly a year or more.[1] Among young minority men, and especially African-American men, the facts are particularly disturbing. For instance,

- as few as 20 percent of black teens are employed at any time;
- among young black men age 16 through 24 not enrolled in school, only about half are working; and
- roughly one-third of all young black men are involved with the criminal justice system at any time (awaiting trial, in prison or jail, or on probation or parole), and a similar percentage will spend some time in prison or jail during the course of their lives.[2]

Why are so many young people "disconnected" from the worlds of school and work, and what can public policy do about it? Much has been written on the problems of disadvantaged youth in schools and in the labor market, and policy at all levels of government has gone through many incarnations.

Yet major problems remain unresolved and many questions remain unanswered. As we show below, recent trends in idleness or disconnection

1

have been worse for young men—particularly African-American men—than for women.[3] And in low-income communities, the incidence of disconnection is much more pronounced than elsewhere.

Long-term disconnection correlates highly with low-income family backgrounds but also with poor future economic prospects—for the individuals themselves, their spouses or partners, their communities, and their children (Besharov 1999). The United States economy can ill afford to have so many of its young people and adults be unskilled, unemployed, and thus unproductive; it cannot afford the high rates of incarceration and child poverty that frequently occur when so many men are without work. And even among men who work full time, skills often remain poor and current and future earnings well below their potential.

Many programmatic responses have proven ineffective when carefully evaluated, and many others have not even been evaluated. More broadly, the youth "system" in the U.S., if it can even be referred to as such, is highly fragmented and serves only a small fraction of youth with extra needs. Under these circumstances, a widespread perception has evolved that very little "works" for disadvantaged youth, a perception some analysts have worked hard to combat (e.g., James 1997), with mixed success.

And yet, well-implemented social policies can succeed. Our recent national experiment with welfare reform showed that states could craft constructive policies that helped raise employment levels and earnings quite dramatically among low-income single mothers, although mothers' poverty rates have remained high (Blank and Haskins 2001). We believe it is possible to change policies and improve educational and employment outcomes for low-income young men as well.

We make no claim to pose or answer all of the questions on disconnected young men. Our focus is on *education and training, broad community initiatives, financial incentives to work,* and special barriers facing *young offenders and noncustodial parents.* Our reasons are briefly discussed here and at much greater length in following chapters.

Our analysis and policy prescriptions reflect our view that the employment problems of disconnected youth reflect both *structural problems* in our economy and society as well as *personal choices.* While declining opportunities and other barriers often constrain youths' choices by creating incentives to disconnect from school and the workforce, personal choices matter as well, and youth must take personal responsibility for their choices. The policies we describe are designed to widen opportunity and encourage or enable young people to beat the odds and become more successful in school and work—but, ultimately, they themselves are responsible for what eventuates.

We do not address all of the critical challenges at length in this book, though all must be addressed for disconnected young people to achieve greater success. First, many members of minority groups continue to experience discrimination (particularly in housing, schooling, labor markets, and the criminal justice system) that can thwart achievement. Our nation and every community within it must continue working to eradicate current discrimination and all vestiges of past discrimination. All laws against discrimination must be fully enforced, and public education and discussion must continue to promote mutual respect and understanding across the fault lines that isolate and stigmatize affected groups.

At the intersection of race, ethnicity, and poverty, other problems disproportionately lengthen the odds of success through childhood—particularly for young people growing up in high-poverty neighborhoods. Prenatal and infant health care are less available and of lower quality. Unhealthy living environments generate higher incidences of disease and chronic health conditions, such as asthma. Schools are far more likely to be overcrowded, have less-experienced teachers, and be of lower quality. African-Americans, especially, are overrepresented in the child welfare and juvenile justice systems and, later on, in the criminal justice system.

At the same time, mass culture glorifies violence and denigrates achievement as measured by conventional norms. Peer culture on the street seems to do the same. Parents fail to read to and otherwise stimulate their young children. Violence is too often the norm for disciplining children and settling disputes within families. Drugs and alcohol have enormous deleterious effects within too many low-income families. The absence of fathers is a negative factor in many homes.

A full strategy to minimize risk of disconnection and maximize positive outcomes for children and youth would include *systemic* attention to children's well-being from the time they are conceived.

Systemic attention would include bolstering the incomes of poor families that include children; encouraging marriage; improving access to health care, child care, and early childhood education; improving low-income neighborhoods, including their schools; and ensuring access to such services as legal assistance, mental health support, and drug and alcohol treatment. Special attention would be paid to children at risk of becoming enmeshed in the child welfare and juvenile justice systems—by preventing their entry into these systems whenever possible and ensuring quality care if a child or youth does become a ward of the state. More fairness in the criminal justice system and an end to discrimination would be critical as well. And we believe that systemic attention would include a variety of public policies and private actions.

Our focus in this book is much narrower than the systemic approach sketched above. But we believe that the areas we discuss are important, and that adoption of our suggestions would make an important difference in improving the educational and employment status of disconnected young men.

Youth Policies in the Next Decade: Our Focus

Our primary focus is on how to improve the educational and employment opportunities available to disconnected young men—with particular concern for African Americans and Hispanics, but not excluding whites. The trends for less-educated young women in both school enrollment and employment have been relatively positive in recent years, and women have been the focus of much attention through welfare reform. Young women are still far from where they should be, but we believe that a focus here on less-educated and low-income men is appropriate. Of course, the policies we review below will not be gender-specific in most cases and can often benefit young women as well as men. But our real interest here is to find policies that will be of particular benefit to disconnected young men.

Based on our review of the causes of continuing employment gaps and idleness among all less-educated men, especially blacks, we have chosen to focus on the following areas of policy in our review below:

- enhancing education, training, and employment opportunities for disadvantaged youth by focusing on individual policy components and on building these components into community systems;
- improving the incentives of less-skilled young workers—particularly low-income men—to accept employment by raising minimum wages or subsidizing earnings; and
- addressing particularly severe barriers and disincentives faced by some disadvantaged youth, such as ex-offenders and young non-custodial fathers.

Our decisions to focus on these three areas derive directly from our review of the data, the research on youth problems, and the policy contexts. For example, the link between low levels of education and skills and the limited employment and earnings of young minorities leads us to emphasize efforts to improve these skills, both for those still in school and those who have left.

We focus on four different components of education and training policy for youth, defined by the youths' ages and the situations they might find themselves in. These four components are (1) youth development policies aimed primarily at adolescents and early teens; (2) high school programs that can better serve the disadvantaged, including career and technical education (CTE, formerly known as vocational education), school-to-career efforts, Career Academies, and alternative (or charter) high schools; (3) community colleges; and (4) second-chance employment and training programs for out-of-school youth. We also consider the current generation of employment-related entities that work to bridge the gap between potential workers and employers. Most such "intermediaries" serve adults, but some serve older youth too.

We begin with adolescents because so much research suggests a need to reach young men relatively early—before they have detached from school or the labor market and run afoul of the law or fathered children out of wedlock. More obviously linking performance in school and job opportunities should help to better motivate boys who currently have difficulty seeing the connection, and perhaps will encourage more of them to avoid engaging in self-destructive behaviors. These links are also important for immigrant boys who often drop out of school because of pressure to support their families.

Regarding high school programs, we focus primarily on improving academic performance and linking young men and women to the job market before they disconnect. Attending college is an important goal, but better policies will not cause everyone to do so; the labor market will continue to offer opportunities to young people emerging from high school with strong occupational skills or solid work experience. Given that so many young black men in particular neither develop these skills nor get early work experience, serious attempts to remedy these failings deserve great attention.

The tight labor market, and perhaps even worker and skill shortages, that will likely be created by baby boomer retirements reinforce our focus on training and work experience. Many employers complain about their inability to hire and retain qualified workers—and many expect these difficulties to grow more serious in the coming decades—so we believe that employers might be motivated to get more involved in training and hiring at-risk youth. But, unlike the first generation of "school-to-work" policies, these efforts must be heavily targeted on less-advantaged youth. The links between school- and job-based training and work experience will also need to be stronger than in "school-to-work" policies of the 1990s. Links should be pursued within the context of CTE as well as newer "school-to-career" efforts.

High school programs that focus on students at high risk of dropping out and invite dropouts to return—often referred to as "alternative" schools—are another avenue for improving skills and educational credentials for the disconnected. Alternative schools come in many forms, though little research is available on their efficacy to date. Programs that blend high school and community college curricula are another area of growing interest we will explore, community college being an opportunity for post-secondary education for many disadvantaged youth who may not be ready for four-year programs. Improving access to community college education for minorities and low-income people is thus on our agenda as well.

Of course, the need will remain for "second-chance" programs for out-of-school youth. We consider current efforts—including Job Corps, the various youth "service corps," YouthBuild, and others—that develop the skills and also the attitudes, values, and behavior of these young men. But, given the multiple "mismatches," persistent discrimination, and weak networks that divide disconnected young men from employers, the need will continue for other approaches that bridge the many gaps.

Third-party "intermediaries"—community organizations, for-profit or nonprofit job placement agencies, or other institutions with close ties to specific industry groups—can often connect young men to employers. The current generation of intermediaries clearly understands the need to treat employers (as well as disadvantaged workers) as their clients, and to win employers' trust by addressing business needs. Intermediaries do so by working closely with employers, providing workers with the skills and behaviors employers seek, and carefully screening candidates for job readiness.[4] A closer look at the potential role of intermediaries in linking disadvantaged out-of-school youth to the labor market—and perhaps to schools as well—is thus advanced.

Our discussion of education and training will not just be limited to the four components of policy noted here. We are troubled that existing policies are fragmented, sometimes duplicative of and even inconsistent with one another. Large gaps typically separate isolated efforts to improve youth outcomes. We do not wish to add to the existing confusion.

We hope instead to encourage the creation of effective youth *systems* operating primarily at the local level but with support and funding from state and federal governments and other sources. These systems would ideally constitute an infrastructure that offers all youth in a local area a full range of educational and training opportunities. Youth systems would aim to involve every relevant local party—including schools; employers; community organizations; faith-based groups; local government; and foster care, child welfare, juvenile justice, and criminal justice system personnel—to create seamless webs of services. Intensive case management might be needed to keep disadvantaged youth actively involved, and incentives might have to be provided to local officials for such tracking.

But youth employment policy must go beyond a focus on education and training. Even with major improvements in education and training programs, the skills and education of many young men from low-income backgrounds will lag behind those of most other youth. Given the economic shifts over the last three decades (which we review in detail in the next chapter), less-educated young men now face fewer job opportunities and lower wages (adjusted for inflation and relative to more-educated workers) than they did a generation ago—and will continue to do so for the foreseeable future. The decline in wages and the related disappearance of blue-collar jobs have clearly reduced the incentives for many young men to enter and remain attached to the legitimate labor market. Declining labor force attachment imposes major costs not only on young men, but also on their families and children, on their communities, and on our nation.

As a nation, we should increase earnings for less-educated and less-skilled young men. Raising federal and state minimum wages, which have eroded in value over time, would help. We also should consider using subsidies or tax credits to supplement earnings. In the 1990s, the nation developed a range of "work supports" for low-wage welfare mothers and custodial parents—including an expanded earned income tax credit (EITC) that subsidizes low wages by as much as 40 percent, and increased child care and health care subsidies.[5] But most of these efforts have little effect on childless young men or those who are noncustodial parents.[6] Efforts to raise or subsidize their low earnings should be part of a comprehensive plan to motivate them. And, where we can identify reciprocal obligations—which were successfully implemented in some states with welfare mothers—we should use them.

Incentives to work appear weakest for the growing number of ex-offenders and noncustodial fathers among young African-American men.

We need special efforts to remove employment barriers and to reform punitive policies that effectively drive many out of the labor market.

What would constitute a complete range of effective policies to combat disconnection is still not fully known. Some rigorously evaluated programs have generated disappointing results, and many more have never been evaluated at all. We will try to be honest about what we do know and what we do not—and where we can only call for experimentation and evaluation rather than full-scale policy implementation.

The Remainder of This Book

The next chapter will present a detailed statistical look at youths' school enrollment and employment rates by race and gender, and review the social science literature on youth employment. We also discuss the economic and political contexts in which youth policy will be made in the coming years. The chapter will elaborate on our focus on the three sets of issues listed above—education and training, financial incentives to work, and barriers facing young noncustodial fathers and ex-offenders.

The rest of the book is organized around these three broad areas of youth policy. Chapters 3 and 4 focus on education and training for youth and on community-wide systems, respectively. Chapters 5 and 6 explore improved work incentives and barriers facing youth offenders and noncustodial fathers. In every chapter we explore the strengths and weaknesses of existing efforts, along with proposals for innovation. We identify the most promising ideas in each area, consistent with our reading of the evaluation evidence and of the likely future policy contexts. We then conclude with a chapter that summarizes and integrates what we have learned and suggests some practical "next steps" that can be taken at the federal, state, and local levels to improve policies for young men.

NOTES

1. "Disconnected" is not a term of art. Other counts of young people who are not employed or in school sometimes generate higher numbers, in the range of 4 to 5 million, though they often include youth who have attended some college. The Annie E. Casey Foundation (2004) concluded that there were 3.1 million disconnected youth age 18 to 24 in 2000, growing to 3.8 million by 2003 due to declining employment rates during that period's recession.

2. The teen employment rate appears in the Bureau of Labor Statistics monthly Employment Situation reports (2005); the employment rate for those age 16 to 24 is documented in chapter 2, while the incarceration figures appear in various publications of the Bureau of Justice Statistics (for example, "Additional Corrections Facts at a Glance," 2005).

3. We define "idleness" as being out of school and out of work. "Disconnection" refers to idleness for at least one year.

4. See, for instance, Giloth (2003).

5. Medicaid extensions for poor children were supplemented by the development of the State Children's Health Insurance Program (SCHIP) in the late 1990s. Other child care and earnings supplements were increasingly funded out of the Temporary Assistance for Needy Families (TANF) block grant during this period, as the welfare caseload and cash payments out of the block grant to families dropped precipitously.

6. Childless adults age 25 to 64 are currently entitled to a maximum EITC payment of $383 per year.

2

The Characteristics of Disconnected Young Men

A Review of Evidence, Literature, and Context

In this chapter, we present some basic statistical facts—about school enrollment, employment, and idleness rates among different demographic groups of youth and among young men versus women. We also review what we have learned from research about the causes of poor labor market outcomes, especially among young African Americans, and what this literature implies for public policy. We briefly consider the U.S. labor market over the next few decades, especially after baby boomers begin retiring in large numbers; and the political and fiscal contexts in which policy decisions will be made.

Some Statistics about Youth Idleness

We begin with evidence on enrollment, employment, and idleness. Several authors have recently provided detailed accounts of the youth population's characteristics (e.g., Sum 2003; Wald and Martinez 2003). Rather than reproducing their results, we highlight some facts that shed light on particular dimensions of the youth problem and what we (as a society) might do about it.

We define youth as those age 16 through 24.[1] We present data from the Current Population Survey (CPS), the monthly household survey administered by the federal government to 60,000 households and used to compute unemployment rates and other statistics.[2] As a survey of households, the CPS focuses on those not in the institutional population—it omits those who are incarcerated or enlisted in the military. As the former have become a growing segment of the youth population, we adjust some of our numbers below to account for differences across groups in incarceration rates.[3]

In table 2.1, we present data on youths' school enrollment and employment in 1999, one of the last years of the 1990s economic boom.[4] We present the fractions of all youth who are enrolled in school (secondary versus postsecondary education), employed but not enrolled, and "idle." We do so separately by race/ethnicity and gender.

Table 2.1. *School Enrollment and Employment Rates for Youth Age 16 to 24, 1999*

| | Men (%) | | | Women (%) | | |
	White	Black	Hispanic	White	Black	Hispanic
Civilian noninstitutional population						
Enrolled	49.0	47.6	36.6	50.8	46.5	38.6
Secondary school	25.3	28.1	23.8	23.4	25.0	22.2
Postsecondary or other school	23.7	19.6	12.8	27.4	21.5	16.4
Employed and not enrolled in school	42.3	29.6	50.6	35.9	31.9	32.6
Idle	8.7	22.8	12.8	13.3	21.6	28.8
Civilian noninstitutional population and incarcerated population[a]						
Enrolled	48.5	44.1	35.6	50.8	46.1	38.6
Secondary school	25.1	26.0	23.1	23.4	24.8	22.2
Postsecondary or other school	23.4	18.1	12.5	27.4	21.3	16.4
Employed and not enrolled in school	41.8	27.4	49.1	35.9	31.6	32.6
Idle	9.6	28.5	15.3	13.3	22.4	28.8

Source: Bureau of the Census, Current Population Survey (1999).

a. CPS calculations were supplemented with summary data on youth incarceration rates available from the Bureau of Justice Statistics at the U.S. Department of Justice.

- *Employment rates among young African-American men lag dramatically behind those of white and even Hispanic men. Their rates of idleness are dramatically higher as well, especially when we account for those who are incarcerated.*
- *Postsecondary enrollment rates are now higher among women than men in each racial/ethnic group. A "gender gap" has thus developed in educational attainment that favors young women over young men. Employment rates among young black women also exceed those observed among young black men—even though many of these young women have childrearing responsibilities.*
- *Hispanic youth are enrolled in school, especially postsecondary school, at much lower rates than white or black youth. And postsecondary enrollments among African Americans lag behind those of whites (as do high school graduations, though the data in the table do not indicate the latter).*[5]

In table 2.2, we present idleness rates, once again for 1999, but this time we focus on youth who, at the time of the survey, had been idle for at least the entire previous year. These are the youth we define as "disconnected" for this book. This distinction is important, since temporary idleness is frequently observed among youth and has far less negative longer-term con-

Table 2.2. *Idleness Rates for Youth Age 16 to 24, 1999*

	Men (%)			Women (%)		
	White	*Black*	*Hispanic*	*White*	*Black*	*Hispanic*
Civilian noninstitutional population						
Disconnected (idle for at least one year)	3.2	10.5	9.3	7.1	9.0	10.4
Married parent	0.2	. . .	0.3	3.1	0.3	3.1
Single parent	. . .	. . .	. . .	1.3	3.2	0.6
Not married, no children	3.0	10.5	9.0	2.8	5.4	6.8
Civilian noninstitutional and incarcerated population						
Disconnected (idle for at least one year)	4.2	17.1	11.9	7.1	9.9	10.4

Source: Bureau of the Census, March Current Population Survey (2000).

sequences than does long-term idleness. In addition, we consider the marital status and childrearing behavior of those who are idle for a longer period; parenting might account for a lack of schooling and employment among some, especially young single mothers. We also present separate rates of long-term idleness for the civilian noninstitutional population—the group on which most published statistics for education and employment are based—and for a broader group that also includes those who are incarcerated.

The results show that full-year idleness, or disconnectedness, rates are somewhat lower than those shown in table 2.1. Still, 10 percent of young black men and 9 percent of young Hispanic men in the civilian noninstitutional population are idle each year by this measure. These idleness rates for young black and Hispanic men rise substantially—to 17 percent and 12 percent, respectively—when we include those who are incarcerated in the population. Furthermore, in this category, long-term idleness rates are lower for young women—around 10 percent for both blacks and Hispanics—than for men in both minority groups. Also, among the noninstitutional population of continuingly idle young women, more than one-third of blacks and Hispanics are parents. In contrast, virtually none of the idle men in any racial or ethnic group are married or has custody of a child.

In other words, *more than one out of six young black men, and nearly one out of eight young Hispanic men, experience long-term idleness without any major childrearing responsibilities.* No doubt many of these young men are active in the casual or "underground" economy, engaged in either legal or illegal pursuits for income. But, if we define productive work as officially reported, steady employment, large fractions of young minority men are forgoing productive work as well as schooling. And the idleness rates have surely been even higher during the labor market downturn of 2001 to 2004.[6]

Although young whites experience much lower rates of long-term idleness than do minorities (at 4 percent of their total populations for men and 7 percent for women), whites also account for a much larger percentage of the overall population. Thus, though the incidence of long-term idleness within the white youth community is much lower than among minorities, *young whites also account for a significant percentage of the overall total.*[7]

How have school enrollment and employment rates among different groups of youth changed over time? In table 2.3, the data show that

Table 2.3. *School Enrollment and Employment Rates for Less-Educated Youth Age 16 to 24, 1989 and 1999*

	Men (%)			Women (%)		
	White	Black	Hispanic	White	Black	Hispanic
1989						
Enrolled in school	35.6	38.3	25.9	32.9	32.2	26.6
Employed among those not enrolled in school	80.2	59.3	77.7	64.1	40.4	44.1
1999						
Enrolled in school	47.3	46.0	34.3	50.1	44.2	34.6
Employed among those not enrolled in school	80.0	50.0	78.4	64.8	52.3	47.4

Source: Bureau of the Census, Current Population Survey (1989, 1990).

Note: Sample includes all youth age 16 to 24 who have at most a high school diploma.

- employment rates stayed constant for less-educated young white and Hispanic men, but declined precipitously for young black men in the 1990s;
- employment rates rose for less-educated young women, especially black women; and
- enrollment rates have been rising for all groups of youth, but especially white and black women.[8]

The decline in employment among young African-American men is particularly troubling, given that their rates of employment already lagged behind those of white and Hispanic men by about 20 percentage points at the end of the 1980s. By the end of the 1990s, this gap had grown to about 30 percentage points. As noted earlier, employment rates among less-educated young black men now lag behind those of black women, even though the latter more often have significant custodial responsibilities. The gap would be considerably wider if the incarcerated were included in these calculations.

And, perhaps most troubling, the declining employment rates of young black men occurred despite the stunning boom in the U.S. economy in the latter half of the 1990s. Indeed, labor markets were considerably tighter in 1999 than they had been in 1989, even though both years were business cycle peaks.

These results seem to suggest that less-educated African Americans are now unaffected by the business cycle, but this is not the case. Historically, blacks have been more severely impacted by economic downturns and more positively affected by recoveries than any other major group. In fact, both Sum (2003) and Holzer and Offner (2002) find that this continues to be the case. Furthermore, Holzer and Offner (2002) find that every percentage-point increase in the local unemployment rate reduces the employment rates of young black men by nearly 3 percentage points. Unfortunately for young black men, the positive effects of the business cycle in the 1990s were swamped by a downward trend in employment that has been ongoing for several decades but seemed to accelerate in the 1980s. Had it not been for the strong economy at the end of the 1990s, young black men's observed employment rates would simply have been that much worse.[9]

The growing gap in employment rates between young black and Hispanic men is quite noteworthy, especially given the lower school enrollment (and presumably completion) rates we find among the latter. But Hispanics in the U.S. are an extremely heterogeneous group that includes the foreign-born as well as natives and also encompasses a wide range of national origins. In table 2.4 we present enrollment and employment rates among less-educated young Hispanics (again, with a high school diploma

Table 2.4. *School Enrollment and Employment Rates for Less-Educated Hispanic Youth Age 16 to 24, 1999*

	Foreign-born (%)					*Native-born (%)*
	Puerto Rican	*Mexican*	*Cuban*	*Other*	*All*	*All*
Enrolled in school						
Men	18.7	16.1	31.7	23.6	18.2	38.2
Women	14.3	14.6	—	17.4	15.3	37.4
Employed among those not enrolled in school						
Men	49.7	75.4	—	66.0	71.6	60.3
Women	16.9	29.6	52.9	51.3	35.8	44.3

Source: Bureau of the Census, March Current Population Survey (2002).

or less) according to whether they are foreign- or native-born and country of origin among the former.

The results show that foreign-born Hispanics' school enrollment and employment are different from those of their native-born counterparts. The foreign-born are much less likely to be enrolled in school; and the men are more likely to be employed, while the women are less likely to be employed than their native-born counterparts. This is consistent with traditional family patterns among immigrants in which men work at high rates while women rear children exclusively.

But, even among the foreign-born, wide variations exist in enrollment and employment rates. For instance, rates of employment are highest among men from Mexico and lowest among men from Puerto Rico. Indeed, it has been noted elsewhere (e.g., Borjas 1996) that employment rates among the latter group are not dramatically higher than those of blacks, while Mexican-American employment rates are considerably higher. Differing outcomes among Hispanic men by nativity and national origin must be kept in mind as we consider policies aimed at youth who are not enrolled in school or employed.

Finally, what do these varying enrollment rates imply about differences in overall educational attainment and associated labor market outcomes? In table 2.5, we present employment rates and real hourly wages for young

Table 2.5. *Employment Rates and Wages for Young Men Age 16 to 24 Not Enrolled in School, 1999*

	White	Black	Hispanic
Employed (%)			
Less than high school	58.2	36.2	55.9
High school	80.0	65.2	75.0
Some college	83.5	81.1	82.7
College degree or more	92.3	77.8	95.9
Real hourly wages ($)			
Less than high school	7.29	6.58	7.03
High school	8.23	7.54	8.66
Some college	8.56	7.11	8.49
College degree or more	10.51	11.37	10.09

Source: Bureau of the Census, March Current Population Survey (2000).

Note: Hourly wages are in 1999 dollars.

white, black, and Hispanic young men not enrolled in school, separately by educational attainment for each group.

The results show quite dramatic differences in employment and earnings outcomes between educational groups, and, with some exceptions, a strong positive correlation between employment and earnings. Employment rates of young black men lag behind those of both whites and Hispanics at every educational level, but the results among high school dropouts are quite stunning. Indeed, *just over a third of young black male dropouts are employed*—a figure that falls below one-third when the incarcerated are included.[10] Real wages of young black men, as well, are less than those of Hispanics and whites within each group, except among college graduates.

The data in table 2.5 also indicate the real cost to young Hispanic men of their relatively low rates of school enrollment and completion. Clearly, Hispanics work at much higher rates than do young blacks; the exact reasons are explored below. They also earn wages fairly comparable to those of young whites *within* each educational category. But young Hispanics' overall labor market outcomes suffer as a result of their much greater concentration in the categories of low educational attainment. The earnings gaps between Hispanics and whites will also grow over time, considering college graduates' earnings grow with experience more than high school graduates' or dropouts' do (e.g., Filer, Hamermesh, and Rees 1996).

Overall, what do these statistics tell us about idle, less-educated youth? We find that the trends for young women are quite positive—their rates of school enrollment and employment are rising. In fact, their rates of enrollment in postsecondary schools now exceed those of young men in each racial or ethnic group, especially among blacks and Hispanics. Of course, at least part of the traditional male-female gaps in employment and earnings remain, but they have narrowed for all groups; however, employment rates are actually higher, and idleness rates lower, among young African-American women than among young African-American men, even though substantial fractions of the women have childrearing responsibilities.

In contrast, employment rates among young African-American men are falling further behind those of white and Hispanic men (as well as black women), especially when we account for trends in incarceration. Young Hispanic men also have somewhat high rates of long-term idleness; and, though employment rates for less-educated young Hispanic men are fairly high relative to other less-educated men, their low rates of educational attainment imply low earnings over their lifetimes. And even young white men have small but significant rates of idleness, which account for considerable fractions of idle youth nationwide.

What Accounts for Our Findings?

Why are trends in enrollment and especially employment so different for less-educated young women than for less-educated young men, especially among blacks? Why do African-American men lag so far behind whites and Hispanics in employment rates, and why did these gaps continue to grow in the 1990s?

The changes in employment activity among young minority women, especially single parents, have been much studied (e.g., Blank and Schmidt 2001). Most analysts attribute these gains to the combination of tight labor markets in the 1990s, the growth of income supports (such as increased funding for child care, the earned income tax credit, and Medicaid extensions) for the working poor who have children, and changes in welfare policies.

However, less-educated men were little affected by welfare policy changes in the 1990s or by the growth of income supports.[11] Instead, the research literature points to a range of other factors that help account for the continuing and growing employment gaps between less-educated men, especially young black men, and other groups. These include

- declining real wages, especially as blue-collar/industrial jobs disappear;
- weak skills from poor schooling;
- spatial "mismatches" and weak networks between workers and jobs;
- persistent employer discrimination;
- the consequences of growing up in neighborhoods with concentrated poverty and in families with absent fathers;
- popular culture and its effects on youths' attitudes and behavior;
- high rates of criminal activity, arrests, and incarceration—which generate very large populations of young men with criminal records; and
- growing enforcement of child support orders.

A variety of structural economic factors, such as technological change and increased foreign trade and immigration, has caused employer demand for labor to shift away from less-educated men since the 1970s (Katz and Autor 1999). These shifts have reduced overall job availability and real wages for less-educated young men.[12] In response, the labor force participation rates of less-educated men in all racial and ethnic groups declined somewhat during much of that time period (Juhn 1992).[13] As real wage growth resumed in the second half of the 1990s, employment rates seemed to stabilize over that decade among white and Hispanic young men. In contrast, employment rates of young blacks continued to decline for additional reasons we discuss below.

Part of the reason for the decline in real wages of less-educated young men over the 1990s was the continuing disappearance of blue-collar jobs, especially in industrial sectors (like manufacturing) that pay relatively high wages. Indeed, William Julius Wilson (1987; 1996) has heavily emphasized the disappearance of industrial jobs in his accounts of declining employment among young black men. Though the concentration of black men's employment in manufacturing was really only true in the Midwest prior to the 1970s, and though declining manufacturing employment can account for only a relatively small share of the decline in real wages for less-educated men, there is some evidence to back up Wilson's claim that the disappearance of industrial jobs contributed to black men's joblessness, especially in the industrial Midwest.[14]

But, as good jobs for less-educated men have disappeared in the last few decades, the importance of education and cognitive skills as determinants of labor-force success grew. Furthermore, despite gains in the 1970s and 1980s, young Hispanic and, especially, black men continue to lag behind whites in measures of cognitive skill, such as test scores—even among those with similar levels of education (Jencks and Phillips 1998). As a result, the economic penalties associated with the "achievement gap" between whites and minorities have grown.

The achievement gap can be seen quite clearly in table 2.6, which presents scores from a basic cognitive skills test administered as part of the National Educational Longitudinal Survey (NELS).[15] The table indicates that black men, even more than Hispanic men, remain concentrated in the lower rungs of the test score distribution.[16] Indeed, over half of all young nonenrolled black men fall in the bottom fifth of the test score distribution, compared to over 40 percent of young Hispanic men. Furthermore, those with low test scores also have the lowest employment rates in each group—and this is generally true even among those with a given level of educational attainment, such as high school graduates or dropouts.[17] The

Table 2.6. *Test Scores and Employment Rates for Young Men Age 16 to 24, 1994*

	White	Black	Hispanic
Test scores (percent)			
Below the 20th percentile	24.5	54.1	41.2
20th to 49th percentile	37.4	30.5	42.2
50th to 79th percentile	27.9	13.3	13.0
80th percentile and above	10.3	2.1	3.6
Employment			
Below the 20th percentile	74.0	47.7	57.4
20th to 49th percentile	78.0	67.2	69.0
50th to 79th percentile	79.7	61.4	77.6
80th percentile and above	73.6	87.3	84.0
Employment, high school graduates			
Below 50th percentile	83.3	71.3	72.5
50th percentile and above	80.8	74.2	79.6
Employment, high school dropouts			
Below 50th percentile	66.3	37.9	53.9
50th percentile and above	69.0	33.9	76.8

Source: National Center for Education Statistics, National Educational Longitudinal Survey (1994).

Notes: Test scores are from a basic cognitive skills test administered as part of the NELS. Our sample excludes students enrolled in postsecondary education, those without 1988 test score data, and those without employment data. Since those enrolled in college are excluded from this sample, the distribution of test scores is skewed toward the bottom (i.e., more than 20 percent of the sample will fall below the 20th percentile, etc.).

correlation between employment rates and test scores among black men is particularly striking.

This correlation and the concentration of young blacks and Hispanics near the bottom of the test score distribution suggest that a considerable "mismatch" remains between the skills sought by employers—especially for jobs that pay well—and those held by young black and Hispanic men. Other data (e.g., Holzer 1986; 1996) confirm that young minority men often fail to attract offers on jobs that pay near- or above-average wages but require significant skills, though the men are often not interested in the mostly low-wage jobs that do not require such skills.[18] In other studies, controlling for education and test scores eliminates large parts of the wage gap between black and white men but somewhat less of the gap in employment rates (Johnson and Neal 1998).[19]

Note that *employment rates among young blacks (and, to a lesser extent, among Hispanics) lag considerably behind those of whites, even when test scores and educational attainment are equal.* In particular, cognitive skill gaps likely do not explain why young Hispanic men have so much higher employment rates now than comparable young black men or why black women have higher employment rates now than young black men. Noncognitive or "soft" skills, such as attitudes, social skills, and the like, have been increasingly cited by employers as an additional source of earnings and employment gaps between young black men and others (e.g., Moss and Tilly 2001).

Our understanding of exactly why gaps in skills persist between whites, blacks, and Hispanics remains limited. It is quite clear from the research that these gaps are a product of unequal education, rather than unequal innate abilities (Dickens 2005). Poorer family backgrounds, racially and economically segregated schools, and unequal school financing each perpetuate poorer education for blacks. But even after accounting for these factors, much of the racial skills gap remains unexplained (Jencks and Phillips 1998) and perhaps might be attributed to such hard-to-measure factors as lack of early childhood stimulation or diminished expectations of success (among parents, teachers, peers, and others). And the causes of the growing "gender gap" in education between boys and girls remain poorly understood.[20]

The data in table 2.6 lead us to a twofold conclusion. First, *educational attainment and cognitive skills contribute heavily to earnings and employment gaps between young whites and minorities,* and must figure prominently in any discussion of policy responses. Improving the ability and the motivation of disadvantaged boys and young men to remain in school and improve their skills remains a top priority. Second, *gaps in early work experience between young black men and others, which appear unrelated to education and basic skills, also develop early and persist over time.*

What are other sources of labor market disadvantage? In addition to the "skills mismatch," a large body of research has focused on the "spatial mismatch" between jobs that are increasingly located in distant suburbs and the continued concentration of black residences in segregated inner-city neighborhoods. Though the mismatch hypothesis has always been controversial, most recent evidence seems to support it (e.g., Ihlanfeldt and Sjoquist 1998). Apparently, young inner-city blacks not only lack easy *transportation* to areas of high suburban job growth, but also *information* about such jobs.[21]

The access of young blacks to jobs, especially good blue-collar jobs, is further reduced by the weakening of informal networks that have always been major recruitment tools for employers. Indeed, young blacks have historically encountered more discrimination when using "informal" methods of job search than more formal ones (Holzer 1987). In contrast, young Hispanics and immigrants have strong informal networks (Falcón and Melendez 2001), which enable them to gain access to good low-skill jobs that young blacks cannot reach.

Of course, informal networks are often encouraged by employers, especially among groups, such as Hispanic immigrants, perceived to be reliable and hardworking. Indeed, employer preferences for Hispanics over blacks, along with Hispanics' stronger informal networks and lesser "spatial mismatch" (due to lower rates of residential segregation), all contribute to Hispanics' higher employment rates, especially in lower-wage jobs; Hispanics' willingness to accept low wages might contribute as well.[22] But the willingness of young immigrants and their children to accept low-wage jobs instead of completing high school and gaining some postsecondary education also suggests that their employment carries a significant long-run cost in the form of lower wages.

The persistence of negative employer attitudes toward blacks, and especially black men, has been well documented in a variety of research studies.[23] Employers fear conflict with young black men, and they complain about poor attitudes toward work and authority. No doubt some of these employers' attitudes reflect traditional negative stereotypes and racism. Still, it is striking that black employers as well as white employers have noted these concerns (Wilson 1996). Complaints about employees' behavior are often more frequent among employers who hire young black men than among those who do not, which tends to undercut the argument that employer perceptions are simply based on completely uninformed stereotypes (Moss and Tilly 2001).

These facts suggest that the attitudes, values, and behavior of young black men might contribute to their poor performance in schools and the labor market. Alienation from mainstream values and institutions seems strong, especially as articulated in the street (or "hip-hop") culture of the young. By at least some accounts, the peer culture of disadvantaged minority youth treats school achievement as "acting white." The gaps between the lofty aspirations of youth on the one hand and the realities of the low-wage labor market on the other might also contribute to these attitudes and behaviors—as does the continuing perception that school performance has little effect on subsequent employment success.[24]

The attitudes and behaviors of young black men have likely been heavily influenced by trends in family structure and neighborhood composition. In the past two decades, the fraction of young black men who grow up in female-headed households and have absent, uninvolved fathers has increased substantially, as has the number growing up in poor and isolated neighborhoods home to few employed adult men. The lack of fathers in poor black households not only reduces incomes and resources for female-headed families, it also curtails supervision of adolescents, destabilizes household structure and location, and results in the absence of positive role models and labor market connections for boys in those families.[25] Early sexual activity among youth and the frequency of teen pregnancies and births reinforces this cycle over time—though the sharp declines in teen pregnancy rates observed in the past decade are a major positive development (National Campaign to Prevent Teen Pregnancy 2004).

Measuring attitude and behavior, and linking them convincingly to schooling and employment outcomes are difficult. Even when such links can be observed, it is difficult to infer *causation*—in other words, whether the attitudes and values of young black men are really driving these outcomes or the attitudes and values are simply a response to the discrimination and poor opportunities young black men face.

But the attitudes and values of young African-American men certainly reinforce their poor employment opportunities and outcomes when they lead to self-defeating behaviors such as poor school performance, little early work activity, and especially participation in crime. As the rewards to legal work declined for most young black men in the 1980s and the rewards for illegal activity (especially the crack trade) rose, more and more young men opted out of the legal labor market in favor of the illegal one (Freeman 1996). Furthermore, increasingly aggressive law enforcement led to high incarceration rates among young black men over the 1990s.

And, while crime rates have fallen significantly in the 1990s, incarceration rates have not. Currently, roughly 5 percent of all black men are incarcerated—12 percent of young black men age 16 through 34 (U.S. Department of Justice 2003). Most estimates suggest that the number of young men on parole or probation is roughly twice the number incarcerated, leading us to conclude that *well over a third of all young black men are under the supervision of the criminal justice system* at any time. These extremely high rates of incarceration and criminal supervision reflect both high involvement in criminal activity among young black men and their tendency to be disproportionately arrested and convicted.

Prisoners are not tabulated in the Bureau of Labor Statistics (BLS) employment rates. But ex-offenders are likely to be counted, which contributes to young black men's poor employment and earnings outcomes. Ex-offenders are less often employed and earn less than comparably unskilled nonoffenders, reflecting a strong aversion to hiring ex-offenders—especially when they are black men—and the limited labor market experience, substance abuse problems, and weak attachments to the low-wage labor market that ex-offenders themselves exhibit. Together these factors seemingly translate to few job offers to ex-offenders, low wages and benefits, and high turnover.[26]

The fraction of young black men who are not currently incarcerated but who have criminal records grew dramatically during the 1990s and now might be as high as 30 percent of all young black men.[27] Furthermore, employers who do not check criminal records tend to hire fewer young black men, engaging in a form of "statistical discrimination" against an entire group when they cannot identify individuals to avoid hiring.[28] As a result, *the growing presence of ex-offenders in the population appears to be a major reason for the continuing decline in employment of young black men in the 1990s, despite the booming labor market.*

A further contributing factor to young black men's declining employment rates seems to be increasingly strict enforcement of child support orders. Roughly a fourth of young black men, and roughly half of those age 25 through 34, are noncustodial fathers. State enforcement of child support orders has grown increasingly vigorous over the past two decades; most states now use a variety of means to identify absent fathers and withhold child support payments from their wages. But the orders set for young low-income men, at $200 to $300 per month, are quite steep as a percentage of their meager earnings, and, if the men are in arrears, states can garnish up to almost two-thirds of their wages per month.[29] The incentives for young noncustodial fathers to work in regular reported employment—as opposed to casual, off-the-books jobs—have been greatly diminished.

By how much have incarceration and child support policies reduced employment among young black men? An analysis by Holzer, Offner, and Sorensen (2005) suggests that rising incarceration rates have reduced labor force participation among black men age 16 through 24 by about 3 percent over the past two decades, though child support has had little effect for this group. In contrast, incarceration and child support have reduced labor force participation among black men age 25 through 34 by about 5 to 6 percent and 4 percent, respectively. About two-thirds of the reduction in labor force participation occurred in the 1990s. Thus, incarceration and child support seem to account for large percentages of declining employment among black men age 25 to 34 and somewhat smaller declines among those age 16 to 24.[30, 31]

We explore the consequences of child support enforcement and incarceration in much more detail in chapter 6. But the data presented here are sufficient to reveal a great irony of social policy in the 1990s: while we now heavily *subsidize* the earnings of low-income working custodial parents through the earned income tax credit, Medicaid, child care subsidies, and the like, we impose the equivalent of heavy *taxes* on the earnings of noncustodial fathers.[32] That single mothers entered the labor market in large numbers in the 1990s while noncustodial fathers withdrew in large numbers is less surprising when viewed in this context and can be viewed as "labor supply" responses to different trends in net wages and benefits.

Overall, the continuing, and even worsening, employment gap between young black men and others reflects a wide range of forces and developments—some continuing from the past, others new. A changing labor market, weak schools and resulting skill gaps, "mismatches" between employers and potential workers, discrimination, fatherless families, isolated neighborhoods, youth culture, and the criminal justice and child support systems all contribute to the disconnection of young men from school and work. Other aspects of the problem, including physical and mental health problems; problems in the child welfare, juvenile justice, and criminal justice systems; language among immigrants; and the like, are also important but beyond the scope of this book.

The Many Costs of Young Men's Disconnection

For young men who disconnect from school and work, the price they pay over the course of their lives, in terms of lost employment and earnings, will be very large. A lack of education will diminish their earnings, while a lack of early work experience will feed into future wage and employment losses.[33]

But young men's disconnection also imposes large costs on others. Those who engage in crime and are incarcerated impose large public safety costs on their communities. State corrections budgets have grown dramatically since the 1990s, while the absence of employment for ex-offenders imposes an economic cost on the nation. Indeed, Freeman (1996) has estimated that these two components of crime together cost the U.S. up to 4 percent of gross domestic product, which would now amount to over $400 billion annually.

The cost to families and children of fathers who are uninvolved and contribute little financially to their families is also high. Poor employment prospects among young men help account for their low marriage rates (Blau, Kahn, and Waldfogel 2000; Ellwood and Jencks 2004; Wilson 1996), which in turn contribute to the high poverty rates of children in single-parent families (McLanahan and Sandefur 1994). Poor work incentives for low-income noncustodial fathers also reduce their ability to provide financial support, and perhaps emotional support and involvement as well (Mincy 2002).

Finally, the loss of employment among disconnected young men—both today and over the course of their lives—will reduce the nation's labor force and ultimately its economic output and income. This will be particularly true when labor markets are tight and employers have difficulty finding workers, which will occur more frequently after baby boomers begin retiring in a few years.

Accordingly, as a nation we need to undertake a range of policy responses and invest some real resources to address young men's disconnection. We focus here on policies that relate directly to the education and employment of disadvantaged youth and adults. But, to emphasize the importance and relevance of our particular focus, we now describe the context—demographic and economic, fiscal and political—in which policy choices for youth will likely be made.

The Policy Context: Demographics and Economics

Before we consider a set of policies to address the problems of youth idleness, it is important to note some elements of the context that will define the policy environment for the rest of this decade and beyond.

The looming retirements of baby boomers will dramatically change the labor market context for relevant policies. As the Aspen Institute (2002) notes in a recent report, virtually all labor force growth over the first two decades of this century will be generated by immigrants. As baby boomers retire, labor markets should tighten in a wide range of occupations and industries—especially those in which immigrants cannot be expected to provide many workers. And, as immigrants constitute larger shares of new workers, the short supplies of workers in occupations requiring more education and skill will be especially pronounced.

Of course, the labor market can adjust to and avoid impending shortages of workers in a variety of ways: through higher wages that draw more marginal groups (such as the elderly, students, and homemakers) into the labor force, through the substituting of capital and technology for workers, and through offshoring.[34] But, assuming that tight labor markets loom in the next few decades, this also creates an opportunity for policies to expand labor force participation among groups of less-educated youth. Since the country can ill afford to have large pockets of idle youth and young adults in the midst of tight labor markets, the case for investing resources in their productivity is strengthened. And employers openly worried about where they will find workers when their employees retire might engage in renewed efforts to build more opportunities to combine schooling and work.

The Labor Market: What Kinds of Jobs Will Be Available to Our Youth?

Higher levels of cognitive skills and postsecondary education are essential for future labor market success. These notions are rooted in evidence that the real wages of workers with only high school diplomas declined over the past 20 to 30 years, especially among men. While some controversy exists about whether *real* wages have stagnated or actually declined—with the answer depending on exactly how we adjust for inflation—there is no question that hourly wages of young men with high school diplomas or less education have not grown much over the past three decades. And their wages *relative* to more-educated groups have clearly fallen as well—with the gap in earnings between high school and college graduates doubling in this time period (e.g., U.S. Department of Labor 1999). Most labor economists have therefore concluded that the demand for college-educated workers has risen more rapidly than supply during this time period, while the opposite has been true for those with only high school diplomas (Katz and Autor 1999).

But does this mean that jobs with decent wages are completely unavailable to those without postsecondary degrees—and that every worker should be pushed to obtain a college education? Not necessarily. Projections from the Bureau of Labor Statistics (U.S. Department of Labor 2004) regarding occupational growth over the decade 2002 to 2012 show the high-earning jobs that will grow most rapidly *in percentage,* such as computer science occupations, will certainly require high levels of education. Other occupations with high job growth, such as janitors, cashiers, and child care or elder care, will require little education but will pay low wages. But a substantial amount of job growth will also occur in occupations that pay reasonably well and do not require a four-year college degree.

Growing health occupations include medical and dental assistants, occupational and physical therapy aides, and licensed practical nurses.[35] Job growth in the craft occupations, both inside and outside of construction, will be strong as well.[36] Computer technicians such as support specialists and database administrators will be in strong demand (with employment growth projected at over twice the national average). And even in occupations with lower skill requirements but relatively better pay, such as truck drivers or construction laborers, the numbers of workers needed will grow at average or above-average rates.[37]

As Cohen and Besharov (2004) have emphasized, even where BLS projects little net new growth of projected jobs, job turnover, particularly associated with baby boomers' retirements, will create a great deal of hiring (much of it representing replacement hiring rather than net growth) in technical, craft, production, and sales jobs over the next few decades.[38] Labor demand is expected to be strongest in occupations requiring high levels of education; but demand should still be strong in occupations requiring only some formal education and training or interactions with customers—that is, occupations in which immigrants are least likely to be able to fill jobs (Aspen Institute 2002).

Do the BLS projections conflict with the evidence of growing relative demand for college-educated workers? Some analysts (e.g., Bishop 1996) have criticized these projections in past years for understating the growth of occupations requiring college degrees. In fact, the BLS has recently revised how it calculates educational requirements for jobs, and now projects much higher demand for college education than they had in previous years (U.S. Department of Labor 2004). Nevertheless, the newer projections still imply that about two-thirds of the net new jobs created over the decade will not require four-year college degrees.[39] They also show that half or more of jobs in rapidly growing occupations paying above the median can be attained by those with less than four years of college.

In sum, a significant fraction of jobs over the next two decades will not require higher education and will pay somewhere near the median earnings of American workers (now about $14 per hour). Even an increasing fraction of jobs not requiring higher education and formal training will require good cognitive and problem-solving abilities: reading, writing, arithmetic, ability to work in teams, and the like (Applebaum, Bernhardt, and Murnane 2003). Many other jobs will be available to those with strong technical skills and work experience. For the large number of college students who begin but do not finish two-year or four-year degrees, alternative education and training tracks based on associate degrees, apprenticeships, or other certifications might be more successful (Grubb 1996).

Furthermore, research still indicates fairly strong economic returns to early work experience (i.e., during high school) and to on-the-job training (e.g., Lynch 1992; Ruhm 1997), even for workers with no more than a high school diploma.[40] Our primary goals for disconnected youth, especially young blacks, with poor basic skills and little early labor market experience should include developing stronger basic cognitive skills, gaining experience and training, and reducing dropout rates. Improving young people's work-related education and training at the middle and high school levels and preventing their early detachment from school and work are where we need to start.

The Context: Fiscal and Political Realities

We have noted that baby boomers' impending retirement may have a strong impact on the labor market. Of course, another impact is fiscal. The need for the federal government to finance its Social Security and Medicare obligations to retirees will generate fiscal pressures that will preclude many other categories of domestic spending. And the huge federal tax cuts enacted in the past few years, in conjunction with rising spending on defense and homeland security, guarantee perpetually large budget deficits, even during the current decade. State budgets have also been very tight during the recent weak economy, but are bound to improve somewhat when the economy recovers over the next few years. Impending recovery raises the prospect that state governments may be more amenable to innovative policies than the federal government.

Other political realities might also limit the public's willingness to expend resources on idle youth. Young black men—especially those who are not working and have been incarcerated or have fathered children out of wedlock—are perhaps the least popular group in America with politicians. The specter of Willie Horton can easily haunt thoughtful and rational discussions about our need to invest in making youth more productive and better parents.

On the other hand, we might learn something from the nation's experience with welfare policy. Though the effects of welfare policy changes on the incomes of single mothers and their families were mixed, public attitudes toward welfare recipients changed. Welfare mothers went from being objects of derision in the public eye to being viewed as worthy of help as they tried to support their families through work. Seeing more single mothers taking jobs (putting aside the combination of factors that led to this outcome) reduced public hostility toward funding work supports for this population.[41]

The welfare story suggests that it is perhaps possible to link young men and noncustodial fathers to the fortunes of their children in the eyes of the public and to require of them some reciprocal obligations that might inspire greater expenditure of public resources on them. And employers' need for skilled workers might also have a positive effect on political support for policies to address their concerns.

Conclusion

We have reviewed statistical evidence and research on youth employment, the large personal and social costs of young men's disconnection, and the economic and political context in which policies affecting youth will be made over the coming years. All support our focus on three policy areas that will improve youth labor market performance: (1) education and training, (2) financial incentives to work, and (3) removing barriers facing young ex-offenders and noncustodial fathers.

The data and literature clearly indicate that young minorities' basic cognitive skills lag behind those of young whites, which contributes to their employment difficulties. The data also show that young blacks' early labor market experience lags behind even whites of comparable education and cognitive skills. A range of other barriers, including discrimination by employers, weak informal networks, and "spatial mismatch," also reduce their access to jobs.

Our review of labor market projections indicates that economic rewards for college diplomas and strong cognitive skills are growing. At the same time, a wide range of jobs will be available at moderate pay over the next decade and beyond for those with strong secondary education and work experience, perhaps along with some modest postsecondary training and certification. The demographic changes we review also suggest that employers' interest in cultivating new sources of skilled workers will grow, especially as their current baby boomer employees begin to retire.

Accordingly, we focus below on programs that reach young people—especially young boys—as adolescents and improve both their basic skills and their ties to employers in the labor market. We also discuss low-income youths' access to community colleges, where postsecondary certifications are often obtained, and to programs for out-of-school youth and adults, where a wide range of barriers to labor market success can be further addressed. Developing community-wide systems for educating and employing our disadvantaged youth—rather than the fragmented set of programs that currently miss so many of them—will be high on our agenda as well.

But the data and literature reviewed above also suggest that more is required than just a focus on education and training. Since wages for less-skilled young men have clearly declined over time, their incentives to work have diminished; many young men have turned instead to crime. After being released from incarceration, and often faced with stiff child support orders, their incentives to work (and even abilities to get jobs) are further diminished. They then face the additional barriers associated with having a criminal record.

Therefore, we also focus on how to improve work incentives among young men who earn little in the labor market. One approach involves raising statutory minimum wages at the federal and state levels, but only to levels that would not risk reducing employers' willingness to hire less-educated youth. We also address how we might extend the earned income tax credit, which has been so successful at drawing low-income single mothers into the labor market, to young men with child support orders or even to childless adults.

Finally, we consider in greater detail the situations faced by young non-custodial fathers and ex-offenders, and discuss ways in which their barriers to the labor market can be lowered. Developing a set of reciprocal obligations and supports between these young men and their families and communities should be an important part of our agenda.

NOTES

1. The statistics for 16- to 19-year-olds are somewhat different from those for 20- to 24-year-olds. But, for the sake of brevity, we look only across the broader age span.

2. For some tables below, such as tables 2.1 and 2.3, we use the Outgoing Rotation Groups of the monthly CPS. In other cases—such as tables 2.2, 2.4, and 2.5—we use the March CPS data only, which include a special supplement on earnings and activities during the preceding calendar year. Though surveys based directly on interviews with youth (like the National Longitudinal Surveys of Youth, or NLSY) generally show higher rates of employment than does the CPS, which is based on a survey of one household member, our tabulations of the most recent NLSY (which began in 1997 with a cohort of 12- to 16-year-olds) show gaps in employment between young white and minority males that are comparable in magnitude to those observed in the CPS data.

3. The CPS also does not include data on individuals serving in the armed forces or those in other institutions, such as hospitals. With regard to young black men, there is also an "undercount" of eligible individuals in most survey data (Bound 1986). The undercount is probably greatest among nonemployed or low-income young men and likely leads us to understate the employment difficulties of this group. Of course, the reluctance of many young men to report casual jobs for which they are paid in cash likely leads to biases in the opposite direction.

4. Presenting data on 1999 enables us to draw comparisons with data from 1989 at a comparable point in the business cycle, as we do below. Other authors (e.g., Sum 2003; 2004) have focused on employment changes for young whites and blacks during the recent economic downturn. But our primary interest here is on secular trends affecting youth, and therefore we focus on data from business cycle peaks. What happens during recessions is, of course, important for public policy; our purpose here is simply to compare apples with apples.

5. There is some controversy about how dropout rates are measured, since some counts of high school graduates include dropouts who have obtained general equivalency diplomas (GEDs), while other measures are based only on those who have reached the 12th grade. Swanson (2004) argues that high school graduation rates nationally are 68 percent, with rates for whites of about 75 percent and for minorities of just over 50 percent.

6. Sum (2004) calculates that one in four black men experienced long-term idleness during 2003.

7. Non-Hispanic whites still account for over 70 percent of the total population in the U.S.; so even small percentages of idleness among white youth will account for significant percentages of overall idleness. In fact, Wald and Martinez (2003) estimate that nearly 40 percent of all idle youth are white.

8. Rising enrollment rates over time could, at least in theory, be partly responsible for declining employment rates among those who remain nonenrolled, since the average ability levels of the latter may be declining over time. But this factor cannot possibly explain why employment trends across racial and gender groups diverged so widely in the 1990s; see also Holzer and Offner (2002).

9. Freeman and Rodgers (2000) emphasized the growth in employment for young black men between the business cycle's trough in 1992 and its peak in the late 1990s. Holzer and Offner (2002) find smaller rates of employment growth from trough to peak and

declines from peak to peak—partly because Freeman and Rodgers focus only on young men living in major metropolitan areas and partly because of discrepancies between the two studies' definitions of employment and enrollment over time. Sum (2003) also provides evidence of greater declines in employment for young minorities during the recent labor market downturn.

10. Up to 80 percent of incarcerated young men are high school dropouts (Bureau of Justice Statistics 2003). Thus, of the 12 percent of all young black men who are incarcerated, about 9 to 10 percentage points are likely to be dropouts.

11. While it is possible that men were indirectly and negatively affected by welfare reform—if, for example, employers replaced low-income men with women who had been welfare recipients—the empirical evidence does not support this interpretation. See Blank and Gelbach (2002).

12. The exact extent to which real wages declined for young men is unclear, because most economists believe that the consumer price index overstates inflation and therefore understates real wage growth over time. At best, the real wages of less-educated young men were stagnant over this period of two decades, and they fell relative to those of less-educated women (Blau and Kahn 1997) and more-educated young workers (Juhn 1992).

13. In the labor market, a shift in demand away from a particular group implies a downward movement along the group's "supply curve." The more elastic (or responsive to wage rates) labor supply is for any group, the lesser its labor force participation in response to falling demand. In chapter 5, we discuss some evidence of elastic labor supply among less-educated young men. Of course, diminished labor demand can also imply decreasing job availability, even at lower wages, for some groups—especially if rigidities in the market keep wages from reaching a new "equilibrium" level.

14. See Bound and Holzer (1993) for statistical evidence on how declining manufacturing employment reduced employment rates among black men. See also Young (2000) for ethnographic evidence on the continuing search for blue-collar work among disadvantaged young black men.

15. We are grateful to Duncan Chaplin and Albert Liu for generating computations using the NELS data.

16. Young white, black, and Hispanic men are concentrated at the lower end of the test score distribution because the distribution was calculated for all students in the NELS, including Asians and women, as well as those who enrolled in college. In contrast, the only groups in this table are nonenrolled young men from the three largest racial/ethnic groups.

17. The data on test scores for high school graduates and dropouts have been computed separately and are available from the authors, though sample sizes in some categories are small.

18. Of course, other groups of young men likely have difficulty generating job offers even at low wages. This is probably most true of those with very serious skill deficiencies, physical or emotional disabilities, or criminal records. We discuss the latter extensively in chapter 6.

19. In Johnson and Neal's estimates based on data from the National Longitudinal Survey of Youth, roughly two-thirds of the gap in wages between whites and blacks can be explained by differences in test scores (using the Armed Forces Qualifying Test); but only about one-third of the employment gap can be explained on this basis.

20. See Offner (2002).

21. In the recent Moving to Opportunity (MTO) program, low-income residents of poor inner-city neighborhoods who were relocated to mixed neighborhoods experienced no significant gains in employment or earnings relative to those in a control group (Katz, Kling, and Liebman 2001). This suggests to us that residential location per se does not drive "spatial mismatch." Instead, low-income residents' lack of transportation and information might well have been exacerbated if these supports were not explicitly provided. In the Gautreaux program, a precursor to MTO, adults who moved to the suburbs had gains in employment—but not wages—and their children did better on several educational measures (Rosenbaum 1995).

22. See Holzer and colleagues (1993) and Holzer and LaLonde (2000) for a more extensive discussion. Hispanics might also be willing to accept jobs at lower wages than young blacks (i.e., their "reservation wages" might be lower). Though research has generated little solid empirical evidence, this is almost certainly true among undocumented immigrants who often work for low wages in cash. But the growth of Hispanic employment in somewhat higher-wage industries such as construction and manufacturing, where such employment has declined for young blacks, suggests that employer preferences and networks play an important role as well.

23. See Fix and Struyk (1993) for evidence of continuing discrimination in hiring against blacks, based on "audit" or tester studies using matched pairs of job applicants with identical education and experience credentials. See also Kirschenman and Neckerman (1991) and Moss and Tilly (2001) for ethnographic evidence on employers' reluctance to hire black men, and Holzer (1996) for evidence based on fractions of job applicants who are hired across groups and geographic locations.

24. See Ferguson (2001) and Wilson (1996) for thoughtful discussions. Also see Cook and Ludwig (1998) for evidence on the "acting white" hypothesis.

25. See McLanahan and Sandefur (1994) for evidence on the effects of female headship on children, independent of the effects of low family income; Wilson has emphasized family structure and neighborhood effects in most of his work as well (1987; 1996). Recent evidence on the effects of family structure on youth behaviors and outcomes, based on new data from the National Longitudinal Survey cohort of 1997, can be found in Michael (2002). Evidence that concentrated neighborhood poverty has real effects on youth behavior and outcomes can be found in Ludwig, Hirschfeld, and Duncan (2001), based on random assignment data from the Moving to Opportunity experiment. Jargowsky (2003) has recently found that the percentages of blacks or poor families living in concentrated poverty declined somewhat in the 1990s but remained above the levels observed in 1970.

26. See Travis, Solomon, and Waul (2001) and Holzer and colleagues (2004) on the many difficulties faced by ex-offenders in gaining employment and making other transitions from prison to noninstitutional life. See also Pager (2003) for evidence from an audit study showing that employers are extremely reluctant to hire black men with criminal records. We discuss employment for ex-offenders at greater length in chapter 6.

27. Freeman (2003) has estimated that 22 percent of all black men have been incarcerated. These rates are no doubt higher for younger cohorts of men, who were heavily affected by the rising incarceration rates of the 1980s and 1990s.

28. See Holzer and colleagues (2004).

29. See Sorensen and Oliver (2002), Primus (2002a), and Holzer and others (2005).

30. This analysis uses micro-level data from the Current Population Survey from 1979 to 2000, which have been merged with data on the percentages of black men incarcerated and on state child support enforcement policies in these years.

31. While the data in this chapter focus primarily on those age 16 to 24, fairly large employment declines have also been observed for young black men age 25 to 34 (Holzer et al. 2005). The negative experiences of those age 25 to 34 might indirectly contribute to the problems of the younger group, if the latter are discouraged by what they perceive among the former.

32. The view that child support payments effectively constitute "taxes" on the earnings of noncustodial fathers is supported in that relatively little of the money is actually "passed through" in many states to low-income families that have received public assistance. This interpretation is also most relevant when emotional bonds and contact between the noncustodial father and his children are weak, so that forced transfers from the former to the latter might be viewed by the former as the equivalent of a tax and might affect his behavior accordingly. See our discussion in chapter 6.

33. See Ellwood (1982), Meyer and Wise (1982), and Neumark and Gardecki (1998) for evidence that early employment losses contribute to later losses of employment and/or wage growth.

34. Indeed, some analysts have voiced fears that offshoring could lead to slack labor markets in the U.S., whose workers would have to compete with much lower-paid workers abroad. In our view, offshoring will be limited to specific industries and jobs in which work can be easily digitized and transmitted via the Internet. We expect the retirements of baby boomers to be a larger factor in most sectors.

35. Over the decade, overall employment growth is projected at 14.8 percent. But health care support occupations are projected to grow at about 35 percent, with medical, dental, physical therapy, and occupational therapy assistant positions growing at rates well over 40 percent. See Hecker (2004).

36. Installation, maintenance, and repair occupations are expected to grow at 13.6 percent, (just below the rate for the overall labor market) while construction jobs should grow just above the national average at 15 percent.

37. Construction laborer jobs are expected to grow at 14 percent while truck driver jobs will grow at 20 percent.

38. Of the 56.3 million positions expected to be filled from 2002 to 2012, over one-fifth are projected to be in construction; installation/maintenance and repairs; production; and transportation. Service and professional jobs will each account for about one-fourth. Management, office, and sales jobs will account for the rest.

39. Earlier BLS projections (e.g., Hecker 2004) implied that nearly 80 percent of net job growth would be in occupations that do not require a four-year college degree.

40. The positive relationship between work during the school year and wages can be observed as long as work is less than 15 to 20 hours per week. Above these levels, it appears that work begins to interfere with educational attainment and performance in ways that outweigh long-term gains. Newer evidence (e.g., Tyler 2003) also suggests that more work during the school year might reduce test scores. But work's effect on young blacks' academic achievement is hard to infer, while its effect on future labor market earnings would likely be quite positive.

41. See Heclo (2002) and Mead (2001).

3

Education and Training Policies

In this chapter, we focus on education and training efforts for disadvantaged and disconnected young men. We are especially interested in their readiness for and links to the labor market. We also believe that strengthening young men's skills and early labor market experiences can help to reduce their involvement in crime and their rates of early (unwed) fatherhood.

Education policy in recent years has concentrated particularly on improving test scores and years of educational attainment among disadvantaged youth. The major federal legislation usually referred to as "No Child Left Behind" (NCLB) focuses primarily on improving test scores between grades 3 and 8. Many high school reforms focus on test scores but also seek to improve high school graduation and college attendance rates.

We do not dispute that the basic cognitive skills measured by NELS test scores have become increasingly important for the labor market success of all workers, including those in blue-collar or service-sector jobs (e.g., Applebaum et al. 2003). And we know that the labor market returns to college education have grown over time and will likely continue to do so. For students who have completed high school or will do so with more support and attention, improving their odds of earning a college degree or some other type of postsecondary certification are important goals.

But we also believe that policies focused exclusively on education are incomplete, especially when it comes to disconnected youth. In the previous chapter, our review of NELS cognitive tests indicates that young African Americans, and especially young African-American men, have much lower test scores than whites (though African Americans' rates of high school completion lag behind whites' by somewhat less). But, at any level of test scores (except at the 80th percentile and above) or schooling attainment, considerably fewer young African-American men than white and Hispanic young men are employed. For young Hispanics, especially those from immigrant families, high dropout rates along with high levels of labor market participation indicate a different problem: how to improve their school performance and attendance while still meeting their families' needs for income. High employment rates for Hispanic youth mask their limited lifetime prospects for wage growth and advancement.

For many young people who have trouble gaining a foothold in the labor market, college graduation is less realistic than attaining strong work skills.[1] For young Hispanics, African Americans, and low-income whites, a myriad of family, school, neighborhood, labor market, and attitudinal factors seems to limit their motivation to achieve in school. The lack of direct connections between employers and high schools—indeed, that employers pay little attention to school performance when they hire young people, despite its correlation with future success—seems to reinforce the misperception among disconnected youth that school is irrelevant to work (Rosenbaum 2001). And, when youth (especially young African Americans) perceive that employment is scarce and limited to low-wage work, their tendency to disconnect from both the labor market and school is exacerbated. The disconnection begins at early ages and is apparently reinforced throughout adolescence.

At the same time, our review of labor market trends in chapter 2 indicates that the coming few years will bring strong demand for workers in a range of occupations—not only those requiring college or postgraduate education, but also many requiring specific occupational training and work experience along with a high school diploma or an associate degree. It seems sensible to target the latter occupations to young people now disconnected from both school and work.

Accordingly, we focus on a number of school and labor market initiatives to address the needs of disadvantaged youth during their transition from adolescence to adulthood. We do not review these initiatives in depth, but rather provide an overview of what we know and do not know about each. We distinguish between descriptive evidence of *outcomes* for program participants and evidence of program *impacts,* which can be generated only through *rigorous evaluations using random assignment or other appropriate statistical methodologies.* We do not discuss such topics as NCLB and school reform generally; the literature is vast and the issues beyond our joint expertise. Nor do we consider the full range of "prevention" programs, or specific populations such as youth in foster care. We thus limit our attention specifically to youths' education and training as they prepare (too often unsuccessfully) to enter the workforce.

A major theme of successful programs is *engagement*—attracting and holding on to participants. Depending on the participants' age and the programs' specific mission, three primary factors contribute to engagement: financial incentives or paid work experience, strong social supports that include caring adults, and the ability to change community or neighborhood norms that undermine motivation to succeed.[2] Also, for many youth, the path from school to work is no longer linear. Some take time off to work and then return to school. Others combine work and education. Many youth do not stabilize their lives until their mid-twenties (Furstenberg et al. 2002).

In this chapter, we review four broad "component" areas of youth education and training policy. These are (1) youth development programs (often targeted toward those age 12 to 16), especially as these programs relate to preparation for the labor market; (2) high school policies and programs related to work, including career and technical education (CTE, formerly known as "vocational education"), school-to-work policies, Career Academies, and other alternatives to traditional high schools for at-risk or failing youth; (3) community colleges; and (4) postschool employment and training programs for youth, such as the Job Corps and YouthBuild. This last area includes discussion of innovative job sector–specific efforts that are generally geared to disadvantaged adults but sometimes help link youth to the labor market.

Finally, we list policy recommendations for improving youths' employment prospects. Some recommendations are aimed at the federal government, others at state or local policymakers. We address (1) how to obtain better outcomes with existing federal funds; (2) possible new programs and funding sources; and (3) how to expand ongoing efforts, whether fully evaluated or exceptionally promising.

The Components of Education and Training Policies for Youth

We review chronologically the components of youth employment policy, beginning with young adolescents.

Youth Development Efforts

That activities during off-school hours can help young people navigate their way to adult economic self-sufficiency and civic connectedness has been understood, at least implicitly, for over a century. Since 1902, 4-H has given millions of youth hands-on opportunities to gain skills in agriculture and home economics. The settlement houses of the early 20th century, created in response to waves of immigration, were directed in part to assimilating children and youth into the economy and the community.

With the "discovery" of American poverty in the 1960s came a renewed interest in supplementing education with out-of-school programs. National organizations like Boys and Girls Clubs and Big Brothers Big Sisters began to focus more pointedly on "at-risk" youth. Local organizations like The Door in New York City and Omega Boys Club in San Francisco came into existence with a specific mission to serve disadvantaged young people. Such programs were intended to empower youth, give them access to health care and counseling, and help keep them out of trouble by providing recreation and some homework help.

In the late 1980s, school-community partnerships like the Beacons Initiative in New York City demonstrated that community organizations could use school buildings during off-school hours to efficiently and effectively attract children, youth, and their families. Formal evaluations have validated such approaches as Big Brothers Big Sisters mentoring and the intense immersion of the Quantum Opportunities Program. Quantum, in particular, offers a range of supports and services after school to disadvantaged youth—including case management, mentoring, tutoring, community service, and cultural awareness activities—for a sustained period of up to five years.[3] Yet few youth development organizations were addressing connections to the workforce.

The 1990s saw a proliferation of "youth development" initiatives in federal policy, foundation activities, and local programs. What researchers and practitioners refer to as "positive youth development" programs metamorphosed politically into a terminology of "after-school" programs—not surprisingly, since the latter term is much more politically salient. With the economy hot and the federal fiscal situation trending toward large surpluses, Congress began pouring money for after-school activities into a Department of Education program called 21st Century Community Learning Centers, which now receives an annual appropriation of around $1 billion. However, almost none of these funds go to programs for middle or high school youth—and most are directed to school systems, not to nonprofits. Most programs involve academic reinforcement and recreation, rather than a youth development strategy that also includes connections to employers.[4] So the developments of the 1990s reinforced the earlier tendency of youth programs to omit work from their agendas.

A consensus is now emerging among many in the youth development policy community as to what constitutes thoughtful policy and program design. Basic youth development principles include, "the goal of all youth thriving; the importance of healthy relationships and challenging activities that endure and change over time; and engaging young people as participants, not merely recipients" (Hamilton, Hamilton, and Pittman 2004). Many would say that the difficulty lies not so much in identifying the elements of program design, but in placing such programs in more communities (with competent people in leadership and program delivery). Analysts would hasten to add that even a well-designed, competently staffed program faces the further challenges of attracting and holding young people's interest and neutralizing the threats that jeopardize their future.

Yet design matters if the goal is to prepare youth for the labor market. Even today, most youth development programs tend to focus on recreational activities, mentoring, tutoring, preventing violence and high-risk behavior, and keeping teens in school. Relatively few concentrate on connecting youth to work or teaching job skills—either "hard skills" like carpentry or robotics or "soft skills" like interviewing techniques or writing cover letters.

The Harlem Children's Zone (HCZ), directed by Geoffrey Canada, is a good example of a collection of youth development programs that include both the traditional foci of youth development and employment preparation.[5] Currently HCZ has 15 centers serving 12,600 people, 7,500 of whom are at-risk children. Because HCZ is comprehensive, we will look at it more fully below when considering youth systems. But its programs do prepare youth for work. Canada, like many youth program directors, believes that it is vital to see that young people have a successful work experience early on. Too many disadvantaged young men grow up without ever having a job. Lacking work experience, they do not know the importance of "soft skills," or even what those skills are, let alone how to acquire and use them.

One key HCZ program is TRUCE (The Renaissance University for Community Education), which fosters academic growth and career readiness for 12- to 19-year-olds through activities that emphasize media literacy. Youth gain video production skills by filming *The Real Deal,* an award-winning cable television program that airs weekly in New York. They also write and produce films that have appeared in national and international film festivals, including the Sundance Film Festival, as well as at conferences, leadership workshops, and museums such as the Whitney Museum in New York. TRUCE also operates a youth-run community newspaper, *The Harlem Overheard,* with a circulation of more than 25,000. Approximately 200 youth participate in the TRUCE program and receive a biweekly stipend for their work. TRUCE also features college preparation support and recently opened a fitness and nutrition center that is partially managed by middle- and high-school students (Harlem Children's Zone 2004).

HCZ's Employment and Technology Center (ETC) focuses on teaching young adults how to compete more successfully in the job market. The ETC, open to adults as well as youth, offers numerous computer classes and a walk-in computer lab with Internet access. On the employment side, ETC has developed a job-readiness and skill-building program for 14- to 18-year-olds enrolled full time in school. Twice a week the participants attend classes in computer, math, reading, and basic job-readiness skills. ETC provides a referral service and one-on-one career counseling, and places youth in internships in health care, computing, and other fields. Approximately 50 youth participate in internships and apprenticeships at any time, receiving a stipend of $50 a week. The ETC recently was awarded a grant by the New York City Department of Employment to improve and expand its youth employment program (Harlem Children's Zone 2004).

The Beacons Initiative is another community youth development model that strives, to some extent, to connect youth to work. Beacons are school-based community centers that offer after-school, evening, and summer programming for children, youth, and families six days a week. Most stay open until ten o'clock at night. In New York, where Beacons began, the sites are substantially funded by the New York City Department of Youth and Community Development and managed by community organizations such as the YMCA or the Police Action Leagues. Since the program started in 1991, more than 80 sites have opened across all five boroughs, with at least one Beacon center in every councilmember's district. The model has spread nationally, with programs in Oakland, Savannah, Denver, Minneapolis, and San Francisco. In addition to academic support, recreational activities, and counseling, school-to-work transition is an essential component. The precise programming at each site is tailored to the needs of the local community and, at least in New York, all sites are required to partner with neighborhood organizations, including schools, police departments, and local businesses, and to include parents in decisionmaking. Many of the New York sites have collaborated with the city's Department of Employment to offer job-readiness training, mentoring, and opportunities to gain work experience and develop job skills (Department of Youth and Community Development 2004).

While the Harlem Children's Zone and the Beacons Initiative provide youth employment and skills training as one component of their larger youth development programs, the Hillside Work-Scholarship Connection (HW-SC) is a model that focuses almost exclusively on connecting youth to college or employment. HW-SC works to increase high school graduation and employment rates among youth in Rochester and Syracuse by providing job-skill training and employment. Founded by Wegmans Food Markets in 1987, HW-SC offers part-time employment and scholarships to motivate students to improve their school performance. The program serves more than 1,300 at-risk youth each year. Participants enroll in grades 7 to 9 and can continue through high school. Generally, they have poor school attendance rates and disciplinary records, are below grade level in standardized tests, and have failed several classes. Applicants must have between a 2.0 and 3.0 grade point average. Approximately equal numbers of boys and girls participate; 74 percent are African-American and 13 percent are Hispanic (Promising and Effective Practices Network [PEPNet] 2003).

The essential elements of HW-SC are weekly mentoring, employment training, job placement, and college preparation. Upon enrollment, participants and their parents or guardians meet with a youth advocate to create an "Individualized Development Plan," which sketches out multi-year academic and career goals. Youth meet weekly with their advocates to discuss employment placement, academic concerns such as improving study skills, and college preparation. HW-SC's career planning and placement curriculum includes academic enhancement, career exploration, job readiness, and social and life skills. All participants must complete the curriculum before being placed in jobs. Mock interviews and job shadowing are available to make job entry less intimidating.

HW-SC also offers apprenticeships; to participate, students must demonstrate job readiness, meet academic standards, and show respect for adults and other youth. HW-SC has more than 30 apprenticeship sites at a range of area businesses. Each worksite provides a mentor to help youth become successful employees. The program also offers SAT preparation, college tours, and assistance with college admission and financial aid applications. HW-SC and several local colleges offer special scholarships for HW-SC graduates (PEPNet 2003).

The Harlem Children's Zone, the Beacons Initiative, and the Hillside Work-Scholarship Connection have all recently generated some evidence on outcomes or plan to do so in the near future. Philliber Research Associates has worked with HCZ since January 2000 to develop indicators against which to measure program performance for both interim and longer-term outcomes. HCZ's web site (http://www.hcz.org) offers some preliminary data on TRUCE and the ETC, but provides no assessment of skills developed or employment outcomes. In 2002, the Academy for Educational Development (AED) and the Chapin Hall Center for Children completed a five-year study of the New York City Beacons Initiative. Additional data have been provided by Public/Private Ventures (P/PV),[6] and the Center for Governmental Research (CGR) recently completed a six-year longitudinal study of HW-SC youth who stayed with the program longer than seven months, which generated some evidence of positive outcomes associated with the program.[7] But none of this evidence to date constitutes a rigorous evaluation of program impacts, based on random assignment or comparable statistical methods.

Still, the models represented by TRUCE, the ETC, the Beacons Initiative, and the HW-SC are promising endeavors to lower a major barrier faced by disconnected youth: their inability to develop sustained connections to the world of work. Other youth development efforts, like Big Brothers Big Sisters and (to a lesser extent) Quantum Opportunities, have less of a labor market focus but have been more rigorously evaluated and have demonstrated at least some positive impacts at a modest cost. Greater study of the more employment-focused projects is clearly needed, but it appears that youth development programs—which can reach young people early enough to prevent their disconnection in adolescence—are an appropriate and potentially important part of a total strategy to generate positive outcomes for disconnected young men.

The High School Years: CTE, School-to-Work, Career Academies, and Alternative Schools

While the process of "disconnection" begins for many boys in early adolescence, the teen years are when disconnection often becomes a reality. Disinterest in school takes hold, reinforced by its apparent irrelevance to the labor market. The large size and impersonal nature of so many high schools, on top of disciplinary problems and violence that reflect (and perhaps contribute to) participation in "risky behaviors" (such as crime, drug and alcohol consumption, and early sexual activity), likely encourage disconnection for low-income and especially minority young men.

Efforts to reform high schools have gained some momentum over the past decade. Specific high school reforms have been proposed recently by President Bush and by the National Governors Association.[8] The basic elements of these school reforms—such as smaller schools, higher academic standards and accountability, support for teacher training and skill development, and greater choice for parents and students—have been included in some well-known efforts (e.g., High Schools that Work, Talent Development, First Things First, The Small Schools Project). But rigorous evaluation evidence remains slim.[9] And many reforms are not targeted at the kinds of low-income or predominantly minority communities where dropout rates are highest and cognitive skills are weak.

We think the following have the greatest potential for improving links between disconnected youth and the labor market: (a) vocational education—now known as career and technical education (CTE); (b) school-to-work policies; (c) Career Academies; and (d) alternative and charter high schools.

CAREER AND TECHNICAL EDUCATION

Most comprehensive high schools in the United States continue to offer CTE. Along with free-standing vocational/technical high schools and local centers, some 13,000 programs serve 11 million secondary and post-secondary students (Association of Career and Technical Educators 2004). CTE enrollments have declined strongly in the past two decades—perhaps reflecting concern about its quality, but also as college enrollments have risen (Cohen and Besharov 2004). Still, vocational education forms a significant part of the educational experience of nearly half of all high school students (U.S. Department of Education 2004). These programs generally combine education in specific occupational categories with some work-based learning or work experience such as cooperative education or internships. Less than 10 percent of the cost of CTE is funded by the federal government—primarily through the Carl D. Perkins Vocational and Technical Education Act (at $1.3 billion annually) but also through other sources, including the Workforce Investment Act (WIA) and the Higher Education Act (for postsecondary students).

CTE has been widely criticized in recent years as having weak academic standards and job training that is out-of-date and unrelated to the needs of the labor market. Many of these criticisms were leveled in the National Assessment of Vocational Education published by the U.S. Department of Education in 1994. In 1998, Congress articulated its priorities for reform when it reauthorized the Perkins Act: bolstering basic academic standards, updating and strengthening the CTE curriculum, and making schools more accountable for student performance and their CTE expenditures. Some recent evidence suggests that the academic content of CTE courses has improved since then (U.S. Department of Education 2004).

But has CTE reform successfully improved student skills and labor market performance? Little consistent research has been conducted on CTE's impacts on education or employment outcomes. Existing cross-sectional research suggests that CTE modestly reduces dropout rates and improves post–high school employment outcomes and earnings (Bishop and Mane 2004; Cohen and Besharov 2004; U.S. Department of Education 2004). But questions remain about the quality of this research. Of particular concern for researchers is that students who choose (or "self-select" into) CTE may differ from students in college preparation or general tracks in ways difficult to control for, generating selection biases on estimated impacts.[10] Given the wide variation in the type and quality of state and local programs, uncertainty also remains about which programs are successful and which are not—and whether programs effectively serve disadvantaged youth in urban or rural areas.

Another limit to the potential success of CTE is the perception among parents and students that occupational training "tracks" students out of college curricula and higher-wage occupations (Brand 2003). A variety of ethnographic and anecdotal evidence suggests that the vast majority of parents and students, even among those failing at the secondary level, still aspire to college attendance. Despite evidence that many vocational students go on to postsecondary education, and despite a lack of evidence that successful programs like Career Academies (which we review below) deter college attendance, a case for occupational training simply has not been made to students or their families.[11]

Given these issues, further CTE reforms have been proposed. For instance, Brand (2003) calls for Perkins to become a competitive grant to support rigorous academic and occupational training beginning in grade 9 and continuing through grade 12. The Bush administration has also recently suggested, although with different details, that Perkins funds be used for high school reform.

School-to-Work

In the 1980s and early 1990s, educators and youth policy specialists began calling for new efforts to prepare youth not bound for college to work. Citing examples such as Germany, where apprenticeships play a larger role in training youth for the workplace, and Japan, where employers are more closely involved with secondary education, these analysts proposed similar efforts in the United States.

The argument for a "school-to-work" thrust rested on four assumptions. One was that "contextual learning" could be more effective pedagogically than classroom education that is more detached from work. A second was that links to the workplace would improve motivation to learn, which is so often absent when students do not see the connection between the classroom and postschool work opportunities. Third, education and training might be more effective and more relevant when directly linked to the needs of employers—and employers could demand curriculum reforms that school administrators or teachers might otherwise not embrace. Fourth, students would gain from better occupational skills and links to employers that would settle them into particular jobs or careers earlier, thereby preventing unproductive "churning" from one job to the next.

Further research has challenged some of these ideas. The extent to which work-based or "contextual" learning is pedagogically superior to traditional classroom learning, or whether such links enhance student motivation, remains unclear. Much (but not all) "churning" constitutes productive job mobility associated with wage growth over time (e.g., Topel and Ward 1992). And studies of the youth apprenticeship system in Germany note drawbacks, including that training is often too narrow for general labor market mobility and success.[12]

Some economists also argue that U.S. employers are willing to train young workers for specific occupations as long as young people arrive with good basic skills and general job readiness. On the other hand, employers' willingness to invest in general training may be limited by the fear that trainees will take their skills elsewhere, or by other labor market uncertainties.[13]

Congress passed the Clinton administration's School-to-Work Opportunities Act (STWOA) in 1994. The Act provided seed money for states and local school districts to improve links between school systems and employers. In operation, however, STWOA initiatives paid little attention to the work-based education and links to employers that already existed, and little effort was made to coordinate the STWOA with older systems.

Critics also charged that the STWOA often generated superficial activities—typically, job shadowing and career fairs—rather than curriculum changes, clarified career paths, or work-based learning. (We note some exceptions below.) More broadly, conservative critics deplored federal intrusion into local education policy. Others worried about "tracking" students out of college early in life, as we noted above. Many school districts were torn between targeting the lowest-achieving half of their students and establishing more universal programs that included the college bound. The latter were often more popular politically but did not effectively target disadvantaged students. Thus, the original focus of the school-to-work movement on youth not bound for college or more disadvantaged youth was often lost.

Yet existing evaluations of the STWOA (summarized in Hughes, Bailey, and Mechur 2001) generally suggest that both students and employers found it worthwhile. Some evidence suggests that program participants had better school attendance rates, took more challenging courses, and achieved higher grades than they otherwise would have. But much of this research suffers from the same limitations regarding selection bias that we noted with CTE.

The STWOA expired in 2001, and no serious work has been done to replace it. Accordingly, some who helped design and implement the STWOA have more recently focused their attention on sustaining the state and local activities it stimulated, with new funding sources, stronger local partnerships, and better public relations.[14]

Others have called for a new initiative to deepen occupational skill building and employer involvement while more carefully targeting students unlikely to get postsecondary training on their own. Lerman (2002; 2003), in particular, has developed models for apprenticeship programs, along with a model pilot program for the construction industry, that would serve these goals. He argues that only apprenticeships would generate sufficient skills and credentials to yield significantly higher earnings for disadvantaged youth over the long run.

The case for expanding apprenticeship training or for funding internships more generously is even stronger. Deeper private employer involvement in apprenticeships should strengthen their quality, since employer-provided training clearly generates higher earnings for workers (Lynch 1992). Budgetary constraints on public funding make the investment of more private-sector funds critical as well. Impending skilled-worker shortages as baby boomers retire might also spur employers and industry groups to take a greater interest. Still, without significant support and technical assistance from the public sector, such efforts are unlikely to develop and be sustained on their own, as a recent GAO report and other research have suggested.[15]

Support for expanding apprenticeships also comes from state activities under the STWOA. For example, Wisconsin spent school-to-work funds on developing a statewide apprenticeship system, which reaches high school students and seems to deliver meaningful occupation training and related classroom education. Students can choose from 21 program areas that range from architecture to biotechnology to lodging management. Employers are trained to mentor their youth apprentices and provide them with the skills and knowledge to find entry-level work in their program fields. Generally, students can complete one- or two-year programs that encompass both work and classes. The one-year architecture program, for instance, requires 450 work hours and two semesters of coursework that includes computer-aided drafting, architectural instruction documentation, and materials and methods of construction. Students who successfully finish earn a certificate of occupational proficiency and can also receive advanced standing in their apprenticeship fields at local colleges and technical schools (Wisconsin Youth Apprenticeship Program 2004).

CAREER ACADEMIES

A rigorous evaluation (based on random assignment techniques) of one school-to-work modality is MDRC's study of the Career Academies model. Some 2,500 Career Academies now operate, funded by money from Perkins and various state sources. The Career Academy is a small school, often housed within a larger comprehensive high school, that mixes traditional academics with training in such industries as health care, financial services, and travel and tourism. The academies have strong links to employers and provide significant work experience. Career Academies, unlike CTE, use a career theme to make school more interesting; but the classes are not that different from others within the school and the curriculum tends to be less interdisciplinary than CTE (Robert Ivry, conversations with the authors, 2004).

In 11 states, some large high schools have reorganized into career academies under the Talent Development High Schools model. Talent Development, which began in Baltimore in 1994, uses Career Academy elements in high schools with high dropout rates, poor attendance, and low academic achievement. The model specifies small learning communities (as does Career Academies) and encourages students to take more advanced English and math classes, while fostering academic supports (such as tutoring), professional development for teachers, and parental involvement.

An MDRC evaluation (Kemple 2004) shows that students in the Career Academies did no better and no worse than those in the control group along any academic dimension. But, over a four-year follow-up period, Career Academy students' postschool earnings were approximately 10 percent higher overall, roughly 18 percent higher among young men. Not only were earnings gains higher among young men than women—reversing the traditional pattern seen in many labor market training programs—but they were especially high for young men at high and medium risk of dropping out of school. Though little rigorous evidence shows Career Academies' long-term effectiveness, MDRC is now planning for another four-year follow-up study.

Exactly why Career Academies have been successful, at least over the last few years, remains unclear. Perhaps their most successful ingredient is simply that they are small schools with a particular theme and focus—something emphasized in many high school reform efforts[16]—or perhaps the links with employers improved subsequent labor market performance more than the curriculum changes did. That students stay with the same group of teachers for two to four years may also make a difference. Career Academies may also increase students' confidence about their skills and abilities. MDRC believes that positive earnings effects are attributable to the high quality of the students' work-based learning experiences and having their employers as references when applying for jobs (Robert Ivry, conversations with the authors, 2004).

The observed positive effects on post-school employment and earnings rather than academics are broadly consistent with findings from any work experience during high school, CTE, and overseas programs (Ryan 2001). The short-term evaluation for the Talent Development High School model (Kemple and Herlihy 2004) also shows positive impacts on course completion, grade promotion, and certain test scores among 9th graders.

Furthermore, that Career Academies generated positive impacts on employment and earnings without any negative impacts on academic achievement or postsecondary enrollment suggests concerns about "tracking" lower-income youth into careers that do not require college are likely overblown. Career Academies, and other successful versions of CTE or school-to-career programs, do not deter young people from pursuing postsecondary educational options. At their best, they should provide strong academic *and* career preparation that will enable young people to choose from a variety of routes after high school.

Thus, Career Academies might be further expanded, as a form of CTE or a model of high school reform more broadly. And high school models with characteristics broadly similar to Career Academies or Talent Development might be expanded as well.

ALTERNATIVE AND CHARTER HIGH SCHOOLS

The failure of high schools in low-income urban school districts, with notoriously high dropout rates and poor student academic performance, has led to the development of a wide range of "alternative school" programs—sometimes within the traditional school systems and sometimes as freestanding charter schools. Alternative schools have been motivated by the belief that failing students might be better served in a separate setting more suited to older dropouts, where teachers can focus on their particular needs.

Public alternative high schools come in many forms and are not easy to categorize.[17] They include district-administered schools that students attend full- or part-time, district-administered schools located within a community organization, charter schools, educational programs within juvenile detention centers, and schools that operate at night or during the weekend (National Center for Education Statistics 2002).

The recent trend toward charter schools has led to some innovative efforts to make high schools more career-oriented. High Tech High School, at the former Naval Training Center in San Diego, opened in 2000 to train students for the "high tech" workforce. Students do not study technology, but instead use technology in all of their classes to learn and demonstrate their skills. The academic curriculum is rigorous, with the goal of preparing students to enter the University of California or California State University. High Tech High School enrolls about 400 students, who apply and are then selected by lottery. Its student body is diverse: 47 percent Caucasian, 18 percent Asian, 17 percent African-American, and 16 percent Hispanic. State-of-the art facilities are offered for project-based learning, and all students are required to complete internships during their junior and senior years for 8 to 10 hours per week. For several years, the school has received the highest ranking on the California Academic Performance Index. The Bill and Melinda Gates Foundation has provided funding to replicate High Tech High in 15 cities across the country (NewSchools Venture Fund 2004).

Another promising public charter school is the Henry Ford Academy (HFA), founded in 1996 by the Ford Motor Company, the Henry Ford Museum, and Greenfield Village on Ford's grounds in Dearborn, Michigan.[18] HFA's curriculum is academically challenging, focusing on math and technology, and prepares students for both college and the workplace. Employees from Ford and other local businesses serve as academic coaches, guest lecturers, curriculum consultants, and career mentors to students in 11th and 12th grade. Students are regularly tested in academic content, technology, communications, thinking and learning, and personal development, the five areas recommended by a panel of Ford Motor Company managers as the most important for success in the 21st century workplace. To graduate, all seniors must complete the "senior masters process" (SMP). The SMP begins with a junior-year seminar that includes four components: (1) learning about self; (2) learning about careers; (3) learning job search skills; and (4) developing a professional portfolio. During students' senior year, they complete at least 75 hours of fieldwork in a career area that interests them. Each student shadows an adult mentor who provides hands-on learning experiences and helps the student research and develop the product. HFA received a grant from the U.S. Department of Education to develop and share its best practices in innovation and community partnerships.

HFA is open to all Wayne County, Michigan, students in grades 9 to 12; admission is conducted by lottery. The school currently enrolls 420 students. Fifty-one percent are male; 65 percent are African-American; 28 percent are white; 6 percent are Hispanic; and 29 percent qualify for free or reduced-price lunch. Around 90 percent of the graduating students have pursued postsecondary education or joined the military. Since the school opened in 1997, the average daily attendance rate has exceeded 96 percent, though over 40 percent of students take public transportation.

Studies by Steinberg, Almeida, and colleagues (2003) suggest that, in particular, the Tech Prep, Early College High School, and Middle College High School programs that combine high school with community college curricula (with opportunities for students to gain postsecondary credentials as well as high school diplomas), and are frequently housed on the campuses of the latter, are encouraging. Some promising examples of such programs are those in Portland, Oregon; Dayton, Ohio; and New York City (the LaGuardia program). But, of the three, only the Dayton program incorporates a work preparation component into the curriculum.

Portland Community College (PCC) has a program called College Bound that enables high school dropouts to earn a high school diploma and a community college degree at the same time. Students must have a 7th to 8th grade reading capacity to enroll. Participants learn in groups of 20, with intensive work at the start, especially in mathematics and English, to bring their skills up to college proficiency. Each student is assigned an "ombudsman," so they receive personal counseling and support for the entire program. The payoff has been high attendance and impressive achievement. PCC also offers an option for students with limited English proficiency (called the Multicultural Academic Program) to get them ready for College Bound, and a GED option for older students with low skill levels (Steinberg, Almeida, et al. 2003).

At ISUS Trade and Technology Prep (ISUS stands for Improved Solutions for Urban Students) in Dayton, Ohio, faculty from Sinclair Community College teach college-level technical courses to mainly high school dropouts who are also taking high school courses and learning on the job from master craftsmen. The construction trades program is associated with the local YouthBuild program; Sinclair faculty teach computer technology and manufacturing technology in two other training programs. Classes are small, students move at their own paces, and the academic content is delivered in the framework of the trade the student is learning. These high-risk students are getting high school diplomas at a rate of 60 percent (Steinberg, Almeida, et al. 2003). A key element of the ISUS strategy is augmenting the educational side of a "brand name" employment program—YouthBuild in this case (Pennington 2003).

The Excel Program, an "early college high school", emerged from two small high schools (Middle College High School and International High School) already housed at LaGuardia Community College in Queens, New York City. Excel is especially designed for immigrants and their children, as well as for students at risk of dropping out from other high schools. The two small high schools have a long track record of delivering literacy skills to at-risk students. Now they are applying their experience and the unique strength of being located in a college in a new way, and it shows promise (Steinberg, Almeida, et al. 2003).

Schools combining high school and community college are often limited by state or local rules that govern curricula at community colleges. They are also more difficult to develop in states where charter schools have less support, or where funds to local school districts (based on "per pupil expenditures" and "average daily attendance") are not easily applied to students in public charter or alternative schools. Also, as Bailey and Karp (2003) note, combined high school and community college programs have generally not been evaluated, even in rudimentary ways.

Some promising elements common to charter and alternative schools include formal partnerships with local businesses, strong academic curricula, small classes, and students working at their own pace. As charter schools become increasingly popular and funds such as vouchers and other public and private resources become more available, new opportunities to connect disadvantaged youth to the world of work emerge. Many charter schools admit students by lottery, allowing for rigorous evaluation using control groups to reduce selection bias.

Community Colleges

Community colleges have played increasingly large roles in recent years as providers of remedial education and training for the disadvantaged. They now provide not only associate degree programs, but also a wide range of occupational and industry certifications, as well as training for apprenticeships and specific local employers (Carnevale and Desrochers 2001; Grubb 1996). The labor market seems to reward these degrees and certificates to a greater extent than other forms of "second-chance" training that might not provide disadvantaged young people with any postsecondary credentialing.[19] In recent years, TANF, WIA funds, and Pell Grants have been used by states and local workforce investment boards to afford disadvantaged youth and adults these educational opportunities. The Bush administration has also proposed a new initiative focusing on community colleges as training providers, although its funding is carved out of other WIA streams.

Disconnected youths' weak academic preparation limits their access to the traditional two-year degree programs at community colleges; but large fractions of community college students—40 percent nationwide and 75 percent in urban settings, according to Kazis and Leibowitz (2003)—now receive remedial education. Also, the motivation and perception gaps that limit engagement in high school make disconnected youth less willing to continue at the community college level. Even when motivated and academically ready to attend, low-income youth and young adults face additional challenges that deter community college attendance, such as lack of full financing, child care needs, and unawareness of available supports and services (Choitz and Widom 2003).

Pell Grants are the primary vehicle by which low-income youth and adults gain financial assistance for attending community colleges. But maximum grant levels have failed to keep pace with the rise in tuition costs (Levin-Epstein and Greenberg 2003); and several restrictions on Pell Grant eligibility—for example, for those incarcerated or convicted of drug offenses—further limit their usefulness. Without changes in federal law to increase the value of grants and remove restrictions, financial aid officers might work with community organizations to create aid packages based on Pell Grants, TANF and WIA funds, and other state and local sources of aid (Choitz and Widom 2003).

And, as the Opening Doors project at MDRC has emphasized, other changes in curriculum might increase the accessibility of community college courses—such as providing a range of course modules and certifications that low-income students can more easily master (Kazis and Leibowitz 2003). The Early College High School programs described earlier in this chapter already extend these opportunities to students who have not yet completed their high school degrees.

Second-Chance Training Programs

Remedial training for out-of-school youth has taken many forms over the years. Among the best-known programs are the Job Corps, which provides academic and occupational training in a residential setting for up to a year; YouthBuild, which stresses work experience through housing rehabilitation in low-income neighborhoods along with some limited training; and the Youth Service Corps and Youth Conservation Corps, which also provide a combination of work experience through local service provision and training. Many other models and programs are currently funded each year through WIA with roughly $1 billion of formula funding administered by the youth councils of local workforce investment boards.

Some sectoral efforts have also been established. Another promising model, not yet evaluated, is the National Guard Youth ChalleNGe Program, an intensive residential development and mentoring program for older youth.[20]

Job Corps requires little attention here. Created in the 1960s as part of President Johnson's War on Poverty, Job Corps is an educational and vocational training program currently serving about 72,000 at-risk youth, ages 16 to 24, with a total annual appropriation of about $1.5 billion. Three stages of training—career preparation, career development, and career transition—help youth develop job search skills, gain technical and academic competency in a career field, and secure a job. Participants also receive a monthly allowance. It has been evaluated positively, both more than 20 years ago and recently by Mathematica (McConnell and Glazerman 2001). As a residential program, Job Corps is expensive, but it is durable and well-accepted. Provided expansion is done with care, it can surely be much larger. It has, in fact, grown over the past decade.

YouthBuild is much smaller, serving about 6,000 young people at any one time, at about 200 sites. Some 25,000 have been through the program, with 60 percent having graduated. Its basic mission is to teach construction skills and build self-confident, functional people. Thirty percent go into construction or related activities, and 15 percent go on to postsecondary education. In all, 75 percent of 900 graduates surveyed in 2004 were either in college or employed at an average of $10 per hour (Hahn 2003).

Each YouthBuild site builds two to ten homes or residential units a year—one thousand a year in all. The East Harlem YouthBuild owns 12 four-story tenements with 200 units. The St. Louis program owns 300 units.

The sites vary from 15 to 300 participants, with smaller programs obtaining better outcomes. Overall, YouthBuild outcomes have been comparable to Job Corps' in recent years. Five of the sites serve only incarcerated people. A few are residential. Every program is functionally a school as well as a job training experience. About 20 have become charter schools, and more are in the process. A waiting list of three to six times capacity exists at any given time. Participants stay in the program from 6 months to 2 years, with the average stay being between 9 and 11 months. One-fifth have been in prison, and more have been adjudicated juvenile delinquents. About 30 percent are homeless upon entering the program. Around half are African-American, a fifth Hispanic. About three-quarters are men. Average reading level at entrance is between 7th and 8th grade.

The "YouthBuild way" stresses teamwork, solidarity, and a commitment to achieve. Personal relationships matter a great deal—peer to peer as well as with instructors. Respect, inclusion, empowerment, and unconditional love are key. "Mental toughness" is an aim. The program begins with a residential stint of one to three weeks—"root camp," not "boot camp," YouthBuild leaders say. The youth often say, "I found a family." There is zero tolerance for violence, selling or using drugs, and drunkenness. People have to show they are serious about changing their lives to get into the program (Stoneman 2003).

There are now 118 Youth Service and Youth Conservation Corps in 32 states, serving 24,000 youth at any one time. Over half come from families in poverty, and about half do not have high school diplomas. Young men are 59 percent of the corps, and young women 41 percent. Funding is around $339 million a year, mostly public dollars, with about 63 percent from state and local governments and about 30 percent from federal sources. Nearly three-fifths of the Corps' activities are in conservation and the environment, and about a quarter are in education, human services, and health (Sally Prouty, conversations with the authors, 2003).

One of the most persistent themes of the job-training literature is that "second-chance" programs for youth are frequently not cost-effective (e.g., Heckman, LaLonde, and Smith 1999; LaLonde 1995). The clearest example can be found in the 1994 Job Training Partnership Act (JTPA) national evaluation of training for adults and youth. In that study, post-program earnings for adults were considerably enhanced by JTPA training, while for youth the same measures showed no impacts at all (or even negative impacts in some cases). Other well-known programs, such as Job Start (the nonresidential version of Job Corps) and the Summer Training and Employment Program (STEP), also failed to show impact on post-program earnings for youth when rigorously evaluated. To some analysts, this implies that employment problems for disadvantaged youth are more intractable than for adults—perhaps because the youth lack maturity, stability, and a desire for self-improvement.

On the other hand, evaluations of Job Corps have consistently shown that it increases participants' postprogram earnings by 10 percent or more. Of course, Job Corps is the most expensive training program, with an annual cost of about $20,000 per participant. The high expense associated with Job Corps has inhibited its expansion, though it is clearly cost-effective—especially when we include among its benefits the reductions in criminal activity and incarceration that it generates.

But evaluations of somewhat less expensive or intensive programs have found positive results as well. For instance, the short-term impacts (i.e., up to 15 months after enrollment) of the Youth Service Corps have been rigorously evaluated (Jastrzab et al. 1997) and showed strong effects on employment, earnings, and arrests. In particular, estimates suggested a return of $1.60 per dollar spent when evaluators included the imputed value of services generated. While many other programs (like YouthBuild) have not been formally evaluated, outcomes on employment and GED attainment suggest positive impacts.[21]

Some training programs for adults could be extended more broadly to youth. These are generally funded through WIA, TANF, and Welfare-to-Work grants, as well as other sources. The most promising are programs with close links to local employers because, as noted earlier, their training is better designed to meet existing labor market demand. The clear availability of jobs for program graduates seems also to improve motivation and persistence among the trainees.

Sectoral training programs are an example. These provide training for specific sectors of the economy, especially nationally or locally growing sectors, and provide jobs with some upward mobility potential for less-educated workers. Thus, sectoral training often targets industries such as health care, long-term care, and financial services, as well as craft occupations with excess demand for workers, such as machinists. The Aspen Institute's (2002) recent report finds many sectoral initiatives encouraging. Rigorous evaluation studies of some sectoral programs are now underway.[22]

Perhaps the best-known training program with sectoral components and strong links to local employers is the Center for Employment Training (CET) in San Jose, California. Founded in 1967, CET provides vocational training in more than 30 industries. Adults and youth take vocational courses, each requiring 30 to 50 hands-on tasks, to gain specialized technical training and job readiness skills before being placed in full-time unsubsidized jobs. In 2002, 75 percent of program graduates were placed in jobs with an average wage of $9.31 per hour. Of those graduates, 87 percent were placed in jobs for which they had been trained. Rigorous evaluation clearly demonstrated CET's positive impacts and cost-effectiveness (Melendez 1996).

There are now 21 other CET sites in six states. A recent evaluation found some successful impacts on young women, especially in sites that adhered closely to the original CET model; results for young men were less encouraging (Miller et al. 2003).[23] But several other promising programs feature at least some of the characteristics of CET and sectoral efforts, including QUEST (San Antonio); Focus Hope (a program to train machinists in Detroit); WIRENet (Cleveland); and the Wisconsin Regional Training Partnership. Programs that link disadvantaged youth or adults with employers often use labor market intermediaries, who train the workers and place them in jobs, while also working with employers to understand their business needs and provide posthire services (Giloth 2003). Some intermediaries go further, and encourage workplaces to build more upward mobility for workers.[24] Employers' willingness to participate in CET and similar programs is often driven by their own difficulties finding qualified workers when labor markets tighten. Their continued willingness often depends on the intermediaries' ability to provide job-ready, effective applicants.

Community organizations in low-income neighborhoods can sometimes play the intermediary role themselves, or work with other organizations whose links to the employer community are better established. The six-city Jobs Initiative of the Annie E. Casey Foundation has grown fairly large at the local level, though it remains to be formally evaluated. A variety of other intermediaries (such as CEO, the Center for Employment Opportunities, in New York and the Safer Foundation in Chicago) specialize in serving hard-to-employ clients, including those with criminal records.[25]

Overall, we find some success among "second-chance" programs for out-of-school youth, and others (that either target youth explicitly or are available to broader populations) look promising but still must be evaluated. Clearly, it is incorrect that "nothing works" for disadvantaged youth. At the same time, working with disconnected young men, considering the long history of unsuccessful and successful programs, is challenging. A particular concern is that many programs for disadvantaged youth lack the resources to hire trained professionals who can help address prevalent mental health needs that include depression, drug and alcohol addiction, and the current effects of past family violence. Attracting and retaining youth also remain major challenges.

Still, we have developed a better sense of what really works and why. But disconnected youth continue to need remedial programs, and more research is needed into successful efforts on their behalf. At the same time, it is crucial to support the development of programs that reach disadvantaged young people while they are still in school, to resolve problems before they take an irremediable toll or, better yet, to prevent them from developing in the first place. A multipronged strategy makes the most sense, given the evidence.

Policy Recommendations

Our review of education and training policies suggests that each of the components we have considered—youth development programs, targeted high school reform, improved access to community colleges, and training for those no longer in school—play an important role for disconnected youth. Youth development and high school programs can reach disadvantaged young people early enough to prevent disconnection from school and work; community colleges provide skills that the labor market clearly values; and postschool training programs afford second chances for the already disconnected. In each case, some programs have been rigorously evaluated and proven successful, and other promising efforts need to be evaluated. Accordingly, we make the following recommendations for policy:

- Funding for "proven" youth programs that have been rigorously evaluated and shown to be cost-effective should be expanded and made more accessible to communities. Pell Grants for postsecondary education should also be more generous and open to more people with criminal histories.
- The U.S. Department of Labor should initiate a new national apprenticeship program, even if federal funding is to be limited. Broad efforts to engage local schools and private employers are essential.
- Promising new efforts that are not yet "proven"—especially in youth development, CTE, and charter and alternative high schools— should be carefully evaluated as part of an active new federal research agenda.

Expanding Proven Programs

We have discussed a number of programs that have been rigorously evaluated and found to be cost effective, including youth development programs such as Big Brothers Big Sisters and (to some extent) Quantum

Opportunities; the Career Academies model of small schools with a career theme, and perhaps other small school models as well (such as Talent Development high schools); and job-training programs such as Job Corps and the Youth Service Corps. YouthBuild is another program with promising outcome data. All of these programs have been replicated beyond their original versions and have achieved some national scale.

Wider application of these programs requires two developments: (1) more funding, particularly from federal sources; and (2) greater use of available or new funding by local communities. The latter goal can be pursued through technical assistance and broader dissemination of research results to local workforce investment boards. But how to implement the former is less clear.

Only Job Corps and YouthBuild have dedicated federal funding streams. For other programs, local providers cobble together funds from multiple sources such as federal block grants (WIA, TANF, Perkins, the Higher Education Act, etc.), state funding sources, and private nonprofits (such as foundations). Federal block and formula grants can be targeted nationally to specific program models only by a congressional set-aside, which is fairly unusual. Competitive grants can be used by federal agencies to reward the use of proven models, but funding is usually quite limited.

We recommend higher federal expenditures on proven efforts, through competitive grants (such as the "Challenge Grants" recently proposed by the Bush administration under WIA) and through funding streams dedicated to specific programs. But, as the National Youth Employment Coalition and its partners in the Campaign for Youth convincingly argue, the combined federal expenditures on youth training are not nearly sufficient to cover all youth who might benefit from them (Stoneman 2003).[26] So any additional youth training expenditures should be from new funding, not be carved out of other existing appropriations. Funding should rise steadily and consistently over time, so that new funds keep pace with developing program capacity.

Since Pell Grants now fund a great deal of training for disadvantaged youth at community colleges, we believe they should also be steadily increased through the Higher Education Act. Various rules currently restricting the eligibility of disadvantaged youth for Pell Grants (such as the prohibition of criminal drug offenders) should be rescinded as well.

We realize that continuing federal budget deficits will constrain extensive new spending for years. But limiting training programs for disadvantaged youth is not a sensible way to balance the budget. Expenditures on training are small relative to the total budget; cutting them will contribute little to fiscal balance. And training programs are potentially important sources of economic growth in an economy with skilled labor in increasingly short supply. Our suggestions that expenditures be increased do not therefore contradict other calls for restoring fiscal balance (e.g., Rivlin and Sawhill 2004).

A New National Apprenticeship Program

The one area where we think a new federal program is justified is that of apprenticeships and internships. A strong case for the program exists—especially given the general success of private-sector training, the need to encourage more expenditures on disadvantaged youth, and a tight labor market precipitated by baby boomers' retirements. The idea of a federal program for apprenticeships and internships is also supported by state programs' success in subsidizing on-the-job training for "incumbent workers."[27]

An apprenticeship and internship program would constitute the next generation of federal "school-to-work" legislation, but with significant differences from the STWOA in the 1990s. For one thing, the program should be administered by the U.S. Department of Labor, especially its new Office of Apprenticeship, Training, Employer, and Labor Services (OATELS), and perhaps in partnership with the Department of Commerce to signal that the program is intended primarily to engage private-sector employers in subsidized training. In our view, some limited federal funds would be dispersed on a competitive basis to states, which would in turn use them (through existing state apprenticeship councils) to subsidize private-sector expenditures on apprenticeships and internships for high school students. Thus, the program would not be modeled on those in Germany and elsewhere, but would be uniquely American—in the sense of being highly decentralized, flexible, and business driven. The expansion of Wisconsin's apprenticeship program with funds from the STWOA is an example.

Unlike the STWOA, apprenticeship and internship programs should explicitly target students in lower-income communities and schools. The program should not be thought of exclusively as an anti-poverty device, since that would limit business interest; yet it should also not be spread across all students universally. To alleviate businesses' concerns about prospective student quality, participation should be based on real academic and work experience standards. This would admittedly reduce the program's impact on "disconnected youth," especially those who have dropped out of high school. But the prospect of better job opportunities linked directly to academic studies might motivate more young people to remain in school, thus preventing some disconnection in the first place.

The initiative should encourage links between apprenticeship programs and existing CTE and school-to-work programs, and should be part of any community's strategy to create a youth opportunity system. The result would create true pathways into the labor market for low-income young people.

An Aggressive Evaluation Agenda

We discussed a number of promising programs that have not been rigorously evaluated, especially youth development programs and charter and alternative high schools for the disadvantaged. We suggest that the U.S. Departments of Education, Labor, and Health and Human Services expand their research and evaluation agendas. A relatively small investment could generate knowledge to guide state and local policymakers for years to come.

Where significant block grant or formula-based programs (such as the Perkins Act) have not been carefully evaluated, the federal government should fund competitive grants accompanied by rigorous evaluations. In other cases, new federal funding should finance such studies. The cost of doing random assignment studies at a large-enough scale to generate policy-relevant knowledge is too high to be borne by private foundations alone.

At the same time, we cannot expect extensive credible evidence to be generated quickly. Sometimes longer-term evaluations generate different results from short-term studies. On occasion, rigorous evaluations of programs not long in operation—and perhaps not ready for study—have generated misleading data, both positive and negative.[28]

Also remember that what constitutes rigorous evaluation is not perfectly clear in all cases. For instance, random assignment methods cannot be used to analyze community-wide systems; and, even for smaller programs or policies, various nonexperimental statistical techniques can yield insights (see, for instance, Heckman et al. 1999). The growing availability of state and federal administrative datasets (based on unemployment insurance earnings data, TANF program data, and the like) that can be linked to one another also creates the potential for new rigorous nonexperimental evaluations to be conducted.[29] Full federal support for developing new datasets, and for statistical exploration of their uses and limitations, is critical.

NOTES

1. Cohen and Besharov (2004) document high dropout rates among young people, especially minorities, who begin college. The high rates of minorities dropping out of high school, especially in our largest cities, are noted in chapter 2.
2. Robert Ivry, conversations with the authors, 2004.
3. For discussions of the Big Brothers Big Sisters evaluation and the early Quantum Opportunities evaluation see Hahn (1999). For the more recent Quantum Opportunities replication study see Schirm and others (2003), which showed positive impacts on high school graduation rates and postsecondary enrollments, but not on school performance or risky behavior. Active participation in the program dropped considerably over the four-year period studied.
4. The 21st Century Learning Centers were evaluated by Mathematica Policy Research, Inc. The random assignment elementary school study and quasi-experimental middle school study only included first year findings and showed mixed results. See U.S. Department of Education (2003).
5. See Paul Tough's article on HCZ in the *New York Times Magazine* (2004). Some material is also drawn from a personal interview with Canada in 2003 and the HCZ web site, http://www.hcz.org.
6. The AED/Chapin Hall study showed that Beacons were distinguished from other youth development programs in fostering competencies that would help youth as adults (Warren, Feist, and Nevarez 2002). The P/PV studies (Walker and Arbreton 2004) also provide some evidence of positive outcomes associated with participation in San Francisco, such as improvements in self-efficacy and effort in school (but not in school performance).
7. Controlling for race/ethnicity, family income, grade point average, gender, and grade level, CGR found that the high school graduation rate of participants was nearly twice that of nonparticipants (61 percent to 31 percent overall and 60 percent to 27 percent for African Americans). Of the HW-SC youth who graduate, 75 to 80 percent went on to some form of secondary education. The study also found that only 25 percent of those participating actually receive apprenticeships—partly because many do not qualify due to low academic performance, but also because there are not enough jobs available for those eligible.
8. See the U.S. Department of Education and the National Governors Association web sites, http://www.ed.gov and http://www.nga.org, respectively (2005).
9. A major exception is the new study of Talent Development High Schools that has been recently released by MDRC, which we discuss in this chapter's Career Academies section. For more discussion of High Schools that Work and other similar models see Bottoms (2003).
10. As Bishop and Mane (2004) note, these statistical biases are likely to be negative when comparing outcomes of vocational education students to those in "college prep";

but, relative to other comparison groups, the direction of the bias is less clear. We should note as well that cross-country comparisons of high school vocational programs also generate positive correlations between postschool employment rates and in-school vocational training among youth (Ryan 2001).

11. Rosenbaum (2001) notes that school officials, like guidance counselors, have also done little to combat the negative popular images associated with occupational training.

12. See Harhoff and Kane (1997) for a skeptical discussion of the German apprenticeship program and its applicability to the U.S. labor market. Ryan's (2001) review of a variety of occupation training programs, including apprenticeship, across industrial countries is more positive.

13. In Gary Becker's original analysis (1975), employers would not pay for general training, since its benefits might well accrue to other employers, but would help pay for training specific to their own firms. Other market failures that might limit employer expenditures on training include capital market imperfections and liquidity constraints that limit what firms can spend, especially in the short run; imperfect information about training's benefit to employers and cost effectiveness; and wage rigidities that prevent employees from paying for training through lower wages. On the other hand, if an employer has more information about worker training and productivity than other potential employers, the employer might be willing to invest even in general training.

14. See American Youth Policy Forum and the Center for Workforce Development, Institute for Educational Leadership (2000) and National Academy Foundation (2000).

15. See U.S. GAO (2001) for a report that criticizes the Labor Department for having generated too few new apprenticeships in recent years. The report discusses employers' reluctance to develop apprenticeships, but also states that effective support from federal or state agencies can help overcome such reluctance. See Bassi and Ludwig (2000) for some case studies on apprenticeships and internships that show short-term benefits that may not be sufficient to cover costs for many employers on their own, implying the need for some public support.

16. See, for example, the Small Schools Project at http://www.smallschoolsproject.org.

17. See Aron and Zweig (2003).

18. See Henry Ford Academy at http://www.hfacademy.org.

19. See Mathur (2004) for evidence that welfare recipients in California who attended community college had substantially higher employment and earnings outcomes than those who did not. But rigorous controls for participant attitudes or cognitive skills are not included here.

20. Hugh Price discusses the National Guard Youth ChalleNGe Program in his foreword to this book.

21. See James (1997) for more description of outcomes for YouthBuild participants.

22. Evaluation plans for some sectoral initiatives are discussed in Aspen Institute (2004).

23. At least one reason for the relatively weak impacts shown by CET in this evaluation is that members of the control group had gone to community colleges in unusually large numbers, especially in the sites located in California. When comparisons were made between the treatment group and those in the control group who had not gone to community college or received other kinds of employer training, the implied impacts of CET appeared much stronger. A 54-month follow-up study will soon be released by MDRC.

24. An interesting example of such an intermediary is Cooperative Home Care Associates in the Bronx, which helps build career ladders for long-term care workers employed in hospitals and nursing homes.

25. CEO puts greater emphasis on transitional three- to six-month jobs for participants than the Safer Foundation or other groups. A random assignment evaluation of CEO is currently part of a study of strategies targeting "hard-to-employ" workers that is being conducted by MDRC with funding from the Department of Health and Human Services. For more on CEO and the Safer Foundation, see chapter 6.

26. Stoneman argues that it would take $12 billion to fund significant training and employment opportunities for the 600,000 youth who need them each year. She estimates that fewer than half this number are served by all current programs.

27. See Holzer and colleagues (1993) and Moore and colleagues (2003) for positive evidence on state programs in Michigan and California, respectively, that provided subsidies to firms for incumbent-worker training. A related idea, advocated by Rob Ivry of MDRC, is for government and employers to share the cost of college tuition reimbursement for entry-level workers (Robert Ivry, conversations with the authors, 2004).

28. For instance, early results on the effects of Career Academies on academic (as opposed to employment) outcomes overstated their ultimate impacts. On the other hand, some evidence (e.g., Hotz, Imbens, and Klerman 2000) indicates that education and training programs for welfare recipients may provide stronger impacts over the longer term than had been suggested in short-term studies. The 21st Century Learning Centers might be an example of a program that needed more time to evolve before an impact study was conducted.

29. For example, the Longitudinal Employer Household Dynamics (LEHD) program now links unemployment insurance earnings data from participating states to a variety of household and employer survey data at the Census Bureau. For more information on this program see the LEHD web site at http://lehd.dsd.census.gov.

4

Building Community Youth Systems

What might make the greatest difference for disconnected young people would be for their communities to ensure them the same opportunities for getting "connected" as everyone else. Connection has to be a reciprocal responsibility, of course. The provision of opportunity must be reciprocated by the assumption of responsibility—on the part of parents and kin, as well as youth. But too many young men grow up in communities that do not fulfill their part of the bargain.

Why do we need comprehensive community-wide "systems" above and beyond the separate policy components of youth development programs, high school reform, improved access to community colleges, and training for those no longer in school? For one thing, too many disadvantaged youth fall through the cracks, disappearing onto the streets or into correctional facilities with nobody to keep track of them or guide them to appropriate services. But where there is no strategy to create a comprehensive network of services, the necessary help will be unavailable. Indeed, as a White House report recently observed, existing youth programs are frequently fragmented, overlapping, and disconnected from one another, sometimes compromising their effectiveness.[1]

A growing body of scholarly literature emphasizes the importance of "neighborhood effects" that exacerbate the effects of individual and family situations on youth outcomes. The Harvard sociologist William Julius Wilson, among others, has argued that the disappearance of work from poor neighborhoods leads to a breakdown of social norms, informational networks, and behavioral routines necessary to ensure the centrality of work in people's lives. In other words, spillovers, or "externalities," affect youth behavior when poverty and unemployment become geographically concentrated, as they have in the United States.[2]

It follows from this line of argument that public policy should comprehensively enhance employment opportunities for all residents of very low-income neighborhoods, not just randomly for individuals within them.[3] Ideally, each relevant geographical and governmental unit or subdivision would have a system for connecting or reconnecting youth to school and work. A management information system should also unite programs and track individual youth.

Existing endeavors fall far short of that ideal, though three categories of current systemic efforts are worth exploring: (1) neighborhood-based private approaches, supported by both public and private funding, that have grown to some scale; (2) citywide initiatives driven by local government; and (3) nationally supported thrusts to spur comprehensive community initiatives. In this chapter, we consider some prominent examples of each. None has been rigorously evaluated, though all seem promising in their own way.[4]

Neighborhood-Based Nonprofit Systems: Harlem Children's Zone

As we noted in chapter 3, Geoffrey Canada's Harlem Children's Zone is the kind of youth development effort that could be part of a comprehensive community strategy to reduce the number of disconnected young men, though to date HCZ has been primarily a neighborhood operation. HCZ is a complex, multifaceted organization that has been in existence for over 30 years and now has a budget of about $24 million, composed of roughly half public and half private funding (Tough 2004). HCZ began as an after-school and truancy-prevention program and has evolved to have 20 separate program elements that include working with parents to strengthen families. As HCZ has become more comprehensive both in the age groups it serves and the services it provides, it has also become more place-based—in other words, focused on 24 square blocks in central Harlem—and more focused on consolidating its activities into a strategic community-building whole. With approximately 88 percent of the 3,400 children and youth who live in HCZ's area participating in at least one program, Canada is now planning to expand to 60 square blocks where HCZ could reach 6,500 young people (Tough 2004).

Besides the job programs profiled in chapter 3, HCZ offers programs to help families nurture children from infancy through early adulthood. Baby College teaches parenting skills to new parents, many of whom then train for ParentCorps, a group that visits other young parents at home to impart good parenting techniques. To prepare four-year-olds for school, HCZ offers Harlem Gems. In the fall of 2004, HCZ opened two charter schools that will eventually reach 1,300 students in kindergarten through 12th grade. HCZ also operates after-school and summer enrichment programs, including two Beacons Initiative programs. Harlem Peacemakers recruits college-age young people to work in schools on violence prevention. The Family Support Center, which provides walk-in assistance to families in crisis, recently opened a medical and dental clinic. Community Pride involves resident- and community-driven organization of tenant associations and block associations to stabilize city-owned buildings and improve their environment (Tough 2004). As HCZ improves its programs and its evaluation and tracking methods, the organization's detailed 10-year growth plan also projects significant geographic, programmatic, and fiscal expansion.

Canada stresses a number of elements key to the success of any neighborhood youth development program (conversations with the authors, 2003). He argues that it is critical to recruit boys at early ages, perhaps 10 or 11, and on their turf, whether they are on the basketball court or on the street corner. Forming and maintaining relationships with young men until they are finished with college or otherwise firmly connected to the adult world, he emphasizes, is extremely important. At ages 15 and 16 in particular, the pull of the streets is exceptionally strong. In Canada's experience, individual programs are not enough because many youth join, then leave, then come back, and then drop away again.

While HCZ is a promising system, it will be more effective as it works with other organizations, both in the neighborhood and beyond. Canada seeks partners within central Harlem (like large churches) and draws on funding from and partnerships with foundations, public agencies, and specialized nonprofits in other parts of the city—all of which could also have their own strategic approaches to disconnected youth.

Citywide Government Systems: After School Matters

A second category of systemic effort is citywide: a committed mayor or city agency head or foundation executive may develop youth initiatives similar to HCZ but on a far larger scale. A good example is After School Matters (ASM) in Chicago. The program is chaired by Maggie Daley, Mayor Richard Daley's wife, a longtime advocate of programs for children who believed that more needed to be done to help Chicago's teenagers. In 1991, Mrs. Daley and Lois Weisberg, commissioner of the Chicago Department of Cultural Affairs, turned an empty city block, lot 37, into Gallery37, an arts center where children could work alongside local artists, gain job experience, and earn money after school. Mrs. Daley's vision was to create a pathway of opportunity for inner-city Chicago youth by bringing them out of their neighborhoods to a safe space where they could find supportive role models who could help them gain professional skills in a field that interested them (Joan Wynn, conversations with the authors, 2004).

Mrs. Daley quickly decided that one site was not enough and brought together the necessary players to expand Gallery37 into the citywide program that became After School Matters (Joan Wynn, conversations with the authors, 2004). Today, ASM is a partnership of the City of Chicago, Chicago Public Schools, the Chicago Public Library, and the Chicago Park District, which work together to create after-school campuses. In addition to offering recreation programs, ASM engages Chicago public high school students in hands-on activities that help them develop marketable job skills in the arts, technology, sports, and communications. Together, schools, libraries, parks, and local businesses have formed programs in 24 neighborhoods (After School Matters 2004).

Students are given classroom training and paired with skilled mentors to earn money as apprentices. For example, 15 employees of Earth Tech, a Chicago engineering firm, worked for eight weeks with young men from Chicago's south side to install a new water main and repair a neighborhood street. Tech37 students are taught computer skills such as web design, animation, software design, and programming. Students participating in Gallery37 work alongside visual, media, performing, and culinary artists and showcase their art across the city. Sports37 participants work with the Chicago Park District and become coaches for younger players, scorekeepers, summer camp counselors, and lifeguards. They also intern in day camps, in health clubs, in hospitals, and with professional sports teams. Creative writing, storytelling, and publishing skills are developed at Words37. A pilot program created by the Chicago Public Schools connects ASM students to local community colleges and technical schools. Students at Tech37, for example, can take classes at DeVry University to get additional technical training and earn college credit (After School Matters 2004).

From early on, ASM was a conscious effort of the mayor's office to build a youth system in Chicago (Joan Wynn, conversations with the authors, 2004). Much of ASM's growth can be attributed to Maggie Daley, who had a bold vision and the right connections to make the program happen. ASM also complements school reform efforts in Chicago, such as smaller high schools and programs to connect businesses and nonprofits to schools.

Of course, there are limitations. ASM is expensive and will become more expensive as it continues to evolve into a citywide program. With ASM transitioning to a neighborhood-based program, neighborhoods now have considerable discretion over and responsibility for their ASM sites. This, too, creates growing pains, as site directors face an uphill battle for public and private revenue to fund their programs. And ASM has not been evaluated to indicate whether it significantly impacts youth outcomes.[5]

Nationally Funded Community Systems: Youth Opportunity

The most recent innovation in youth training policy nationally is the Youth Opportunity (YO) program. In 2000, the U.S. Department of Labor funded youth programs (or YOs) in 36 low-income sites across the country.[6] YOs were designed to be comprehensive neighborhood efforts to build systems serving disadvantaged youth, expanding on earlier efforts such as Youth Opportunities Unlimited and Youth Fair Chance. The goals of the YO program are to improve current and long-term employability and earnings and raise high school graduation and college attendance rates. (Erik Butler, conversations with the authors, 2003).

The program serves both in-school and out-of-school disadvantaged youth; about 52 percent are, in fact, in school while they participate. The target population is 14- to 21-year-olds, although the pilot programs focused on 16- to 24-year-olds. Overall, about 95 percent of participants are minorities (African-American, Hispanic, Native American, Native

Hawaiian, and Asian). In the neighborhoods where YOs operate, typically only 40 percent to 50 percent of out-of-school youth are working, and school dropout rates are 50 percent. Neighborhoods must have a minimum of 30 percent poverty to qualify for the program. All YOs are in Empowerment Zones or Enterprise Communities, as designated by the Clinton-era programs of those names; 24 are urban, 6 are rural, and 6 are in Native American communities. Grants average $6 million annually, ranging up to $11 million. Most of the grants were renewable annually while the YO program was being funded (Erik Butler, conversations with the authors, 2003).

YO is not just one program, but a collection of programs. All have centers—typically, urban YOs have two or three—where youth can participate in activities and receive counseling and case-management services. YOs are operated by different lead agencies in different cities, such as United Way in Birmingham and the longstanding multicity Hispanic job-training program SER in Detroit. In some places the agency is a Workforce Investment Board, and in others it is another local public agency. At each YO site, case managers—approximately 1,200 nationwide—work with youth individually to set academic and employment goals and provide mentoring, tutoring, and college and career exploration. In some cities, case managers are assigned to targeted schools; in other cities, case managers work at the lead agency (Erik Butler, conversations with the authors, 2003).

Programs and services differ across YO sites, as well. Baltimore has two YO sites, which specialize in training and placing youth in food service, hospitality, customer service, and telemarketing. Baltimore's YO also focuses on dropout prevention and contributes to a college-bound program in partnership with community colleges and Morgan State University. In Memphis, participants who meet job-readiness goals can get paid internships in clerical and support positions at local businesses and community colleges. After 15 weeks, most participants can continue as unsubsidized employees. Participants can attend counseling and support groups for alcohol and drug prevention, take parenting classes, participate in community service, join the YO choir, and compete on YO teams in basketball, chess, and video games. In Moloka'i, Hawaii, where unemployment is approximately 16 percent, the YO program offers training and work experience in forest conservation and fish pond preservation. To receive a stipend, Moloka'i YO participants must attend high school or GED classes; stipend level is linked to attendance, productivity, and work quality.

Some YO sites have formed relationships with their state's juvenile justice system. In Louisville, YO case managers work with youth before they leave a juvenile corrections facility, and youth can serve alternative sentences in the YO center. In Denver, the YO center is a site for serving school suspensions. Memphis, Hartford, Los Angeles, the South Bronx, Moloka'i, rural Arkansas, and Louisiana YOs are regarded as particularly promising (Erik Butler, conversations with the authors, 2003; David Lah, conversations with the authors, 2003).

Like the Harlem Children's Zone, YO aims to be pervasive enough to reduce negative peer pressures against educational attainment and mainstream economic participation; it enrolls about a third of the youth in its neighborhoods. About 80,000 have been enrolled, about equal numbers of girls and boys. During 2003, YO program sites placed about 1,600 to 1,700 youth each month in subsidized and unsubsidized jobs and further education.

As for evaluation evidence, some YO pilot program sites have been studied by Westat (2001). In Houston, employment for out-of-school 16- to 24-year-olds in the target area went from 50.9 percent to 56.7 percent over three years. In the South Bronx the increase was from 24.5 percent to 39.8 percent. These improvements were considerably greater than those observed nationally in high-poverty neighborhoods during the same period.

But, like ASM and HCZ, rigorous evaluation evidence on the YO sites themselves does not yet exist. Furthermore, as emphasized by an Aspen Institute report on comprehensive community initiatives (Connell et al. 1995), no widely accepted statistical methods have been developed for evaluating youth systems. When programs target individuals, they can be randomly assigned to treatment and control groups, thereby eliminating self-selection effects that might bias estimates of impacts. But when systems are designed to benefit everyone who resides in an area, the relevant control group is not apparent; comparable neighborhoods that might serve as controls may evolve differently, especially if local economic conditions or policy environments vary.

Thus, researchers may not be able to develop consensus on a system's impacts, even when evaluations are undertaken. (However, some progress has recently been made, especially with MDRC's evaluation of Jobs-Plus employment programs for urban low-income public housing residents.)[7] At the same time, given the severity of young men's disconnection and the need for solutions, such uncertainty should not be paralyzing.

Forming Community Youth Systems

How should mayors or other local officials who would like to develop systemic approaches to youth schooling and employment proceed? It may not be too simplistic to say that development could begin with a grid in which the age of the clientele is one dimension and the needs of various at-risk subgroups are the other. A grid with all squares covered by responsive and effective policies and programs would be a comprehensive system. System infrastructure—including case management, information systems that track individuals, and the like—would have to be included as well.

The first priority in any youth system with special emphasis on the disadvantaged is public schools. The more children and youth who are served successfully in mainstream schools, the less need there will be for costlier and possibly less successful interventions down the road. We have noted that Career Academies, various other small-school models (such as Talent Development), alternative and charter schools, and the most promising examples of career and technical education and school-to-work efforts are especially relevant for youth, but their context should be a strategy in which effective schools are the centerpiece.

What happens in the off-school hours is vital as well. Much attention has been paid to after-school programs for children, but a closer look reveals little systematic attention to after-school activities for high school students, especially programs that build connections to the labor market. A few cities—Chicago, Boston, and New York with its Beacons Initiative school-based community centers are examples—have approached the off-school hours strategically, partnering with neighborhood nonprofit organizations to create constructive programs. But even cities that have taken after-school programs seriously have paid less attention to older youth; helping them bridge the gap to the job market, for example, would have to become part of any off-school-hours initiative. Furthermore, programs such as HCZ do not spring up with $24 million in funding overnight; HCZ took 30 years to become what it is today. But many smaller models in other locations also remain to be examined.

A mayor or civic leadership group could do worse than replicate the ideas discussed in this chapter. These represent proven, or at least promising, models for youth at all ages and with all needs and histories. The Job Corps, YouthBuild, the Conservation and Service Corps (and perhaps other elements of AmeriCorps), community colleges, and other training programs all include exemplary sites that could be replicated in other communities. These programs, along with a case management and information system infrastructure, could add up to an impressive strategy for building connections to the job market for youth otherwise at great risk. Creativity in adapting these models to local needs is vital too. No "cookie cutter" will produce the same result everywhere.

A mayor, county executive, or governor who wants to create a youth system must call together educational leaders, employers, unionists, foundation executives, key civic and religious figures, judges, juvenile and adult corrections officials, child welfare and foster care officials, social workers, and youth themselves—all stakeholders in better futures for young people. However, that such a convening would result in a comprehensive, community-wide strategy fully operative in the near term is unlikely. Tough decisions will need to be made about where to invest limited dollars: whether to spread resources evenly across a municipality or demonstrate an intensive effort in a few neighborhoods. Creating a 10-year plan and nearer-term objectives will take time and an immense amount of energy. Funding the initiative and attracting and retaining competent staff leadership are enormous challenges. The ongoing efforts of Youth Opportunity sites to sustain themselves, despite the disappearance of their federal funding, are instructive.

A community could begin taking responsibility for its youth through its government, its civic leaders, a nonprofit, or a foundation. Presumably a city- or countywide government initiative would focus on neighborhoods with high concentrations of at-risk youth, but neighborhood organizations could, as Geoff Canada has, take the initiative themselves to bring a community youth system to fruition. They would need outside cooperation in a variety of ways, especially financial, but it is not imperative or inevitable that the effort comes from a government authority. A foundation could also be the catalyst, seeking a city, county, or neighborhood ready to unite its youth development programs in a comprehensive system. Numerous examples of neighborhood foundation initiatives exist, although few relate to youths' transition into adulthood.

Any type of organization could take the lead in forming a neighborhood youth system. It could be a school or a set of schools. It could be an organization with a mission to serve children, youth, and families. The system can grow out of a community housing and economic development corporation, a community health center, a child care center, a drug abuse prevention program, or a domestic violence and rape crisis center.

Lack of funding, of course, could impede a broad local effort. Nevertheless, substantial federal funding is already flowing into communities through block grants and formula grants—although it is true that money is already committed to grantees who would oppose its reallocation, and that funds may be allocated by the state, the county, or a specially created independent body rather than the community. Nonetheless, many federal programs could be tapped: the Workforce Investment Act; Temporary Assistance for Needy Families; 21st Century Community Learning Centers; No Child Left Behind; various Justice Department, Health and Human Services, and Housing and Urban Development block and formula grants; and even the Department of Agriculture's venerable 4-H program (Eccles and Gootman 2002). State and local public funding is possible as well, as evidenced by initiatives in some places. Foundations are another possible source.

All of that said, additional federal funding will be essential to build local initiatives into community-wide systems. We offer suggestions in the following policy recommendations.

Policy Recommendations

All levels of government can encourage building community youth systems in a variety of ways. Government should provide new funding and technical assistance to local Workforce Investment Boards and Youth Councils, help YO sites generate funds to continue their operations, and apply lessons learned from Youth Opportunity, such as their innovative management information systems and case-management techniques. Other public policies can facilitate disconnected youths' inclusion and retention in schools and training programs. Local communities must have better *incentives* (or fewer disincentives) to improve case management and keep young people engaged in productive activities. For example, critics charge that the No Child Left Behind Act creates incentives for school systems to drop their worst-performing students to improve average test scores. States should also revisit funding formulas that reduce per-pupil allotments when students leave traditional school systems for alternative education.

To attract and keep youth, education and training programs should be made more accessible to low-income, minority (especially immigrant), and disabled populations. As MDRC has pointed out, measures can include increased funding for low-income students, more flexible classes and degree programs, and counseling and support services (Choitz and Widom 2003).

Practical knowledge from Youth Opportunity about developing community-wide systems must not be lost. YO operated only for five years, too short a time to establish successful, sustainable systems in areas of concentrated poverty. Many YO sites are just hitting their stride after initial missteps and learning experiences.[8] Others are well-established but in severe jeopardy now that YO funding is discontinued. For literally decades, youth policy experts have called for comprehensive systems in low-income areas. YO is the most extensive attempt ever. To lose it now would be extremely unfortunate.

Possibly the Challenge Grants proposed by the Bush administration can be of some value, especially if they are not funded by cuts in the youth portion of the Workforce Investment Act. Grants could be used to fund a new generation of demonstrations and evaluations that build upon YO's success—perhaps by being wider in scope (e.g., encompassing entire cities or different neighborhoods within large cities), or by involving local employers and educational institutions to a greater extent. But the same goals could be achieved if the YO program itself were restored and expanded, building on its strengths and accomplishments.

A long-term federal funding strategy to assist communities in building youth systems should consist of two basic mechanisms: a formula grant with sensible performance criteria, oversight, quality control, and accountability that could strengthen (or even replace) the current youth title of WIA; and an expanded YO program in the form of a competitive grant administered by the U.S. Department of Labor. This expanded YO program would be separate from the apprenticeship program recommended in chapter 3.

Neither new grants nor YO suffices by itself. A competitive grant program, by definition, will only serve a few communities, but youth systems must serve the entire country. Indeed, the competitive approach has an inevitable political weakness manifested over the past four years—only the people who receive the grants care about continuing the program. Nonetheless, competitive grants are vital for developing best practices and should be saved.

On the other hand, formula grants can sometimes promote waste and a lack of accountability. The success of formula funding depends greatly on performance measures and incentives such as cuts in funding when the money is not well spent. But, as we have learned from the WIA experience, developing measures and incentives is controversial and difficult, though critical to formula federal grants for local system-building.

NOTES

1. See White House Task Force for Disadvantaged Youth (2003).

2. See Wilson (1996) for a general argument about the importance of neighborhood effects, and Jargowsky (1997) for evidence on the growing geographic concentration of poverty during the 1970s and 1980s and its implications for youth behavior. Some, though not all, of this concentration was reversed during the 1990s.

3. The empirical evidence concerning neighborhood effects on youth employment has been somewhat mixed; for a review see Ellen and Turner (1997). But the literature is plagued by several well-known statistical problems. For a convincing study that finds important neighborhood effects when using random assignment data from the Moving to Opportunity project, see Ludwig and colleagues (2001).

4. Another neighborhood project not described here is MDRC's Jobs-Plus Demonstration, an effort to locate employment services within public housing projects.

5. Some data on outcomes for ASM participants (though no formal impact evaluations) are available from the Chapin Hall Center for Children in Chicago.

6. Youth Opportunities funding from the Department of Labor was originally authorized in 1999 for five years at $250 million per year. An original group of 36 grantees in 2000 was to be followed by another round of grantees chosen in 2003. But funding for the latter was cancelled by the Bush administration.

7. In their Jobs-Plus evaluation, MDRC chose cities with two or more public housing projects and then assigned these projects to either the experimental or control groups. They also used administrative time-series data on employment outcomes prior to random assignment to infer the outcomes that would likely have been observed in the absence of the program. See Bloom, Riccio, and Verma (2005).

8. A meeting of YO directors sponsored by the U.S. Conference of Mayors in January 2004 discussed these lessons and YO's future. Some of the conference's themes can be found in Crigger (2004).

5

Improving Financial Incentives for Low-Wage Work

As noted in chapter 2, the last thirty years have not been easy ones for less-skilled low-wage workers, especially men. Relative to other workers, earnings of those at the bottom of the wage distribution have clearly fallen further behind. Worse, in absolute terms, low-income workers' wages have either stagnated or declined, and employment has declined. It is reasonable to believe that reduced incentives to work are one major factor in the decline in employment.

The extent to which declining wages have led to lower employment among young men, and what policymakers might do about it, is the subject of this chapter. We begin by presenting some additional evidence on the wage and employment trends of less-skilled young men and women, and we argue that declining wages have caused some less-educated men to withdraw from the labor market. Then we consider two sets of policy options for dealing with this problem: (1) increasing the minimum wage, which would directly raise the earnings of many young workers; and (2) subsidizing their earnings through publicly provided wage subsidies or tax credits, such as the earned income tax credit (EITC).

Wage and Employment Trends among Less-Educated Workers

In considering wage and employment trends among less-skilled young men and women over time, we focus on all age groups—not just the young—because people's expectations of the wages they will earn in the future likely influence their employment and schooling decisions. In any event, wage trends among younger men are not greatly different from those among men more broadly (Katz and Autor 1999).

Comparing wages over time is tricky because there is no one agreed-on method for adjusting for inflation. The obvious approach is to deflate wages over time using the consumer price index (CPI), but most economists now believe that this overstates the inflation rate for low-wage work. We adopt the alternative of adjusting by the CPI minus one, which involves subtracting a percentage point from the CPI each year in calculating the inflation rate.

Table 5.1 shows the average real wages of full-time male and female workers over thirty years when we deflate by the CPI minus one. For male high school dropouts, wages declined by 18.4 percent between 1970 and 2000, whereas for those with a high school education (but no more), they declined by 4.7 percent. By contrast, wages for men with some college rose by 3.4 percent, and for those with bachelor's degrees went up by 21.2 percent. Among female workers, wages rose at all levels of education, although the largest increases were among more-educated

Table 5.1. *Full-Time Workers' Hourly Wages by Educational Level, 1970–2000*

	1970	1980	1990	2000	1970–2000 (% change)
Dropouts					
Male	$10.26	$9.61	$8.19	$8.37	−18.4
Female	$5.60	$5.77	$6.14	$6.41	14.5
High school graduates					
Male	$12.16	$11.84	$11.17	$11.59	−4.7
Female	$6.99	$7.52	$8.17	$9.13	30.6
Some college					
Male	$13.25	$12.61	$12.58	$13.70	3.4
Female	$7.85	$8.11	$9.52	$10.99	40.0
Bachelor's or higher					
Male	$17.13	$16.58	$19.05	$20.77	21.2
Female	$11.29	$11.06	$14.13	$16.10	42.6

Source: U.S. Decennial Census, Public Use Microdata Samples (1970–2000).

Note: Wages are in 2000 dollars.

workers. Women still make less than men, but the gap is narrowing. Among high school dropouts, for instance, women made 45 percent less than men in 1970, but by 2000, the gap was down to 23 percent.

These trends are mirrored in the changes in employment that appear in table 5.2.[1] While employment dropped among men at all levels of education from 1970 to 2000, the declines are much greater among those who are less educated. Among high school dropouts, for instance, men's employment went from 56.6 percent in 1970 to 42.3 percent in 2000, a drop of one-quarter. For men with a high school degree, the drop was 22.9 percent. For those with some college and those with a bachelor's degree, declines were 7.3 percent and 6.3 percent, respectively. Among women, by contrast, employment rose in every category except high school dropouts, with the largest increases among those with the most education.

In sum, less-educated men are now working less and making less when they work. In 1970, male dropouts worked at the same rate as women with a bachelor's degree, and made only 9 percent less per hour. By 2000, they made 48 percent less, and their employment rate was 30 percent lower. Juhn's work (1992), among others, clearly suggests that this relationship is at least partly (though not completely) causal—with declining wages leading to declining labor force participation among less-educated men.

Table 5.2. *Employment Rates for Men and Women, 1970–2000 (percent)*

	1970	1980	1990	2000	1970–2000 (% change)
Dropouts					
Male	56.6	48.8	41.8	42.3	−25.3
Female	26.1	25.7	24.0	25.4	−2.7
High school graduates					
Male	87.6	79.9	74.3	67.5	−22.9
Female	46.6	52.4	53.4	50.1	7.5
Some college					
Male	79.7	79.2	77.4	73.9	−7.3
Female	46.6	57.7	65.4	64.5	38.4
Bachelor's or higher					
Male	86.8	85.9	85.5	81.3	−6.3
Female	56.7	65.1	73.2	71.8	26.5

Source: U.S. Decennial Census, Public Use Microdata Samples (1970–2000).

Instead of working, what are these men doing? Some are involved in illegal activities, as can be seen in the incarceration numbers, which mushroomed from 340,000 in 1970 to just under 2 million in 2000. Others work off the books—street vending and bartering—with hours of work and wages not reported to the Internal Revenue Service. Such employment does not provide any of the fringe benefits, legal protections, job security, or regularity that, to varying degrees, accompany more formal work. Many men in these situations simply work less, making ends meet by reducing their family responsibilities, either by not marrying or by scrimping on their child support. We address crime and underground employment at greater length in the next chapter.[2]

While the causal link between lower wages and reduced employment seems plausible, it is by no means inevitable. If wages decline, workers could react by working more to maintain total income. On the whole, though, that is not what happens among low earners. According to Lawrence Katz (1998), for instance, a 1 percent wage decline on average has been found to result in a 0.4 percent drop in work by low-wage workers. In the jargon of economists, this implies that the supply of labor is fairly "elastic" with respect to real wages among low earners. Indeed, Juhn, Murphy, and Topel (1991) suggest that work effort is more elastic among low earners than among higher earners.[3] According to Jeffrey Grogger (1998), the decline in employment is closer to 1 percent for each 1 percent decrease in legal earnings relative to potentially available illegal earnings.

An additional piece of evidence on this issue is the impact of the earned income tax credit (EITC) on work effort. After the EITC was expanded in the 1990s, the work effort of low-wage single mothers, its primary beneficiaries, greatly increased (Ellwood 2001). Obviously, much else was changing during this period—welfare reform, child care expansion, an improved economy—so the EITC does not deserve all of the credit, but there is no question it played an important role.

Another example is provided by Canada's Self-Sufficiency Project (SSP). In the SSP, long-term single-parent welfare recipients in New Brunswick and British Columbia were offered half the difference between their actual earnings and $30,000 if they left welfare and found a job working at least 30 hours a week.[4] Over 6,000 low-income single parents participated in the randomized experiment, in which half continued to receive welfare and half received the income supplement. The supplement was available for three years, but only to those who stayed off welfare and worked full time. The result was a 15 percent increase in work effort—30 percent of the treatment group worked full time, compared to 15 percent of the control group (made up of those not offered the supplement). On the other hand, the improvements in earnings for the treatment group did not persist after the supplements ended (Card and Hyslop 2005), which suggests that these supplements need to be permanent in order to affect behavior positively in the long run.

Both the EITC and the SSP initiative were designed for single mothers, so there is a legitimate question whether this evidence is relevant to low-income men—some of whom are involved with drugs or crime—for whom a modest wage supplement may not be much of an inducement to turn their lives around. However, the New Hope project is encouraging. New Hope was a random-assignment study involving 1,357 low-income Milwaukee residents, both receiving and not receiving welfare (one-third of the sample was not receiving welfare). All people in the sample lived in the same targeted low-income neighborhood and had incomes below 150 percent of the federal poverty level. Members of the treatment group were guaranteed a job, an earnings supplement, subsidized child care, health insurance (if not insured), and other support services. All were required to work at least 30 hours a week and were eligible for up to three years. For our purposes, what is significant is that men's work effort increased more than women's, in both hours worked and earnings (Bos et al. 1999; Huston et al. 2003).

Policy Options: The Minimum Wage vs. Wage Subsidies and Tax Credits

As we consider two approaches for raising the earnings of the less skilled, raising the minimum wage versus issuing wage subsidies and tax credits, it is briefly worth summarizing their relative strengths and weaknesses. The minimum wage directly raises the wages of the lowest earners in the labor market. It costs no public money (except for the wages paid to public-sector workers), and therefore is relatively unaffected by the very tight U.S. budgetary environment. On the other hand, imposing a mandate on private and public employers increases the costs they incur when employing youth—which could reduce their tendency to hire young people, even as the latter choose to work more. In other words, mandating a rise in the minimum wage could potentially reduce the *demand* for youth labor, even while raising its *supply.* The minimum wage also has a relatively modest reach, since it only affects the bottom decile or so of all earners (though much higher percentages of youth).

Unlike the minimum wage, publicly financed wage subsidies or tax credits generate no negative effects on labor demand while likely increasing labor supply among youth. The EITC has already successfully raised the earnings of low-income single mothers. But the EITC is costly to the federal budget—current annual federal expenditures are over $30 billion per year—and state earned income credits generate additional public costs.[5] In our policy recommendations below, EITC extensions would not be targeted on youth—though we expect that the employment behavior of young men as well as adults would improve if these proposals were implemented (expectations of future rewards almost certainly affect the education and employment decisions of young people). Political opposition to *refundable* tax credits—those that generate tax benefits to low-income families paying little or no taxes—has risen somewhat in recent years. And we imagine that opposition to providing taxpayer-funded credits to adults without custody of children will be even more substantial. Furthermore, phasing out the subsidies or credits too quickly as earnings rise could reduce net wages and work incentives, as well as low-wage men's and women's incentives to marry. Thus, both the minimum wage and public subsidies or tax credits for low-wage workers have their advantages and disadvantages.

The Minimum Wage

The federal minimum wage currently stands at $5.15 per hour. It was last raised in 1997. In addition, 16 states currently have their own minimum wages set above the federal statutory level.

Since the late 1940s, the statutory federal minimum wage has been raised eight times.[6] After each such increase, the real (i.e., inflation-adjusted) value of the minimum—and its value relative to average wages in the economy—tends to erode until the next statutory increase. But increases have been occurring less frequently, and they have not kept up with inflation or rising wages.

For example, each minimum wage increase from the late 1940s through the 1960s set the minimum at 50 to 60 percent of the average hourly wage of production workers in the U.S. labor market (Chasanov 2004). But the 1996–97 increase set the minimum at just about 40 percent, as did the increase in 1990–91. Furthermore, the minimum has now eroded to under one-third of the economy-wide mean hourly wage for nonsupervisory workers (which stood at $15.86 as of November 2004)—its lowest ratio in nearly five decades.

As the relative value of the minimum wage erodes, it covers fewer workers. Currently, only about 3 million workers—or just over 2 percent of the labor force—are paid the statutory minimum. But recent proposals to raise the minimum (over two years) up to $7.00 per hour would directly raise the wages of all workers in the $5.15–6.99 range, which currently includes over 7 million workers. An additional 8 million in the $7.00–7.99 range might also benefit as their employers strive to keep their wages above the statutory minimum (Chasanov 2004).

Who are the workers covered by the increases in the minimum wage? Overwhelmingly, they are young workers. Indeed, a majority of those earning the minimum wage or just above it are 16 to 24, and 30 percent are teenagers. While the exact percentage rises and falls with demographic factors (such as the baby boom, baby bust, and immigration rates), minimum wage workers are always disproportionately young. Minority workers are more represented as well, even though well over half of those earning minimum wage are white.[7]

Of course, many of those working at minimum wage are not from disadvantaged families. Large fractions are middle-class youth or adults who are the second earners in their households. On the other hand, minimum wage increases tend to disproportionately benefit workers in lower-income families. Thus, the Economic Policy Institute calculates that nearly 40 percent of the higher earnings generated by an increase in the minimum wage would accrue to workers in the bottom 20 percent of income, while 60 percent would accrue to those in the bottom 40 percent (Chasanov 2004).

The greatest concern is that raising the minimum wage might reduce employment among youth, particularly those with the least education or skill. The standard textbook model of labor market supply and demand suggests that any attempt to raise wages above their "equilibrium" level will reduce employment, even though raising wages increases the supply of low-wage labor; that is, better wages presumably generate a surplus in the quantity of labor supply greater than what the market demands.[8] The exact amount of employment loss will depend on the "elasticity" of labor demand among employers—on the extent to which hiring rates are sensitive to the wage rate.

On the other hand, labor market imperfections might offset reductions in labor demand that occur in response to a higher minimum wage. Young people's turnover out of low-wage jobs might also be reduced, thereby further diminishing net loss of employment.[9]

In the end, the effect of a higher minimum wage on youth employment is an empirical issue. Historically, most studies have found small negative effects of the minimum wage on youth employment—for example, a 10 percent rise in the real value of the minimum might reduce youth employment by 1 to 2 percent (Brown 1999). Recently, Card and Krueger (1995) have challenged the notion that minimum wages reduce employment at all, while others (such as Neumark and Wascher 2000) continue to find small negative effects.

The effects of future minimum wage increases on employment will depend on a number of factors, such as the labor market's tightness and demographics like the presence of teens and immigrants in the workforce. We do not believe that the minimum wage increases of 1996–97 generated any loss of employment for youth, since the late 1990s labor markets were so tight (Bernstein and Schmitt 1998). Similarly, given the likelihood of generally tight labor markets over the next few decades as baby boomers retire from the workforce, we do not regard the risk of lower employment rates associated with modest increases in the minimum as being very great. Indeed, we believe the potential of moderately higher minimum wages to keep disadvantaged young men from "disconnecting" more than outweighs the risk of losing employer demand for these workers.

How high can the statutory federal minimum wage rise without jeopardizing the demand for low-wage workers? An increase to $7 per hour, as recently proposed by Senator Edward Kennedy (D-MA) and Congressman George Miller (D-CA), would raise the minimum to just under 45 percent of the mean hourly wage for production workers. This increase is below the typical relative level of federal minimum wage increases throughout the 1950s and 1960s. Yet, given the shifts in demand away from less-educated workers (see chapter 2) and the general decline in less-skilled workers' wages, some long-term decline in the minimum wage's relative value seems unavoidable. At the same time, future increases should be planned to prevent the increase's relative rate from eroding substantially over time. Alternatively, the new minimum might be indexed to the average production worker wage at a moderate level, to prevent erosion automatically.

Thus, we propose the following:

- The federal minimum wage should be raised to roughly 45 percent of production workers' mean wage and should be roughly maintained over time; and
- if the federal statutory minimum is not increased soon, we encourage states to do so on their own—particularly as labor markets tighten.

Policy Options: Wage Subsidies and Tax Credits for Low Earners

To increase the earnings associated with low-wage work, we could subsidize low wages for a broad range of workers; alternatively, we could enact specific expansions in the existing earned income tax credit (EITC). One possibility would be to provide a wage subsidy for *all* low-wage workers, regardless of family income or circumstances. Edmund Phelps (1997) has advanced such a proposal, but his plan was never taken seriously, partly because of the cost, and partly because it was a relatively new idea not well understood by the public. Phelps's notion was that low-wage workers would receive an hourly subsidy of $3, with the amount tapering off as unsubsidized wages rose (the subsidy phased out at around $12 per hour).[10] For those with the lowest earnings, the plan would offset much, if not all, of the wage decline of the last thirty years, depending on how much of the subsidy is passed on to workers (as opposed to being captured by employers paying lower wages).

The cost was estimated at $120 billion, although Phelps argued that it could be recovered from savings in other programs. This seems like an optimistic assumption. Some obvious savings can be identified—the earned income tax credit could be eliminated (for savings of $35 billion), and there would be savings in food stamps and unemployment compensation (Phelps estimated these at $20 billion in 1997)—but beyond that, savings are less clear. Phelps projected welfare and public safety savings on the assumption that low-income people would work more and commit fewer crimes, but these are mere speculations. So while as much as half the cost could possibly be recaptured from other programs, the rest is little more than a guess.[11]

Another way to help low-wage workers is to expand the earned income tax credit, a well-established antipoverty program that has bipartisan support on Capitol Hill.[12] The EITC has one other major advantage: it is targeted to low-income families, while Phelps's proposal is not. Any wage subsidy—even one targeted at low-wage workers—helps those who are not in low-income families as well as those who are.

There are opposing arguments, however. The EITC tends to create marriage penalties because benefits are phased out as family income rises, so two-earner families are more likely to find themselves above the phaseout range (Phelps's plan also includes a phaseout, but his does not depend on other family members' earnings). As noted below, there are ways to mitigate these problems, but they cost money. And the larger the subsidy, the more costly the remedies.

We have developed a proposal for an EITC for single and childless workers (including noncustodial parents) at about 40 percent of the level currently available to individuals with custody of their children.[13] The credit would equal 20 percent of the first $7,500 of annual earnings, which means that the maximum credit would be $1,500 (this compares to a maximum credit of $4,204 for families with two or more children). Twenty percent is roughly equal to the total tax rate paid by single and childless workers if we add Social Security (FICA) taxes and sales taxes. In effect, we would be rebating to low-income workers the taxes they pay. An individual working full time for a year at the current minimum wage would receive $1,400. An individual working three-quarters of the year at $8 per hour would receive $1,120. The credit would phase out at about $20,000 (see table 5.A.1 in the appendix to this chapter).

Estimating the cost of such a credit is difficult because we do not know how many people would file for it. Currently, roughly 90 percent of eligible parents are estimated to participate in EITC, whereas participation in the existing childless credit is 39 percent. If we assume that participation in the new credit would be near the midpoint of this range, or 67 percent, the annual cost is $8.6 billion. Since we are particularly interested in younger workers who are still in the process of making their major life choices, we could limit the credit to 21- to 45-year-olds (and we could also reduce the amount of money going to college students, which is probably desirable).[14] This reduces the cost to $4.3 billion.

There is still the problem of marriage penalties. Suppose the mother and father of a young child are living separately, and each is making $10,000 a year. Using the current EITC phase-in and phaseout rules in table 5.3, the custodial parent would be eligible for a credit of $2,547 and the noncustodial parent for $96. If the parents get married, the credit falls to $1,704 because the family enters the EITC phaseout range. If we add in the new credit for childless individuals, the problem is exac-

Table 5.3. *Earnings and Tax Credits in the Current and Proposed EITC*

	Current EITC		Proposed EITC
	1 child	2+ children	
Earnings required for full credit	$7,500	$10,510	$7,500
Begin phaseout	$13,730[a]	$13,730	$10,000
Phase-in rate (%)	34.01	40.00	20.00
Phaseout rate (%)	15.98	21.06	15.98
Maximum credit	$2,547	$4,204	$1,500

Source: Urban Institute calculations using Urban Institute–Brookings Tax Policy Center data.

Note: The proposed EITC is for childless and single workers, including noncustodial parents.

a. For single-parent families. In two-parent families, phaseout begins at $14,730.

erbated. If the mother and father continue to live apart, the noncustodial parent would receive $1,500 and the custodial parent $2,547 for a total of $4,047, but if they marry, they only receive $1,704.

The marriage penalty problem is not as bad as it sounds. First, when considering federal income tax rules as a whole, most low-income people are better off getting married than remaining single. Even with the current EITC marriage penalty, for instance, the parents described in the preceding paragraph would be better off by $186 if they married (see table 5.A.2 in the appendix to this chapter). If their earnings differ—let's say the noncustodial parent earns $16,000 and the custodial parent earns $4,000—the federal tax benefit if they marry and file a joint return is $3,342 (see table 5.A.3). Second, even where our EITC plan does create a marriage penalty, some relatively simple steps can be taken to ease the problem. For instance, we could allow two-earner families to earn more than one-earner families before benefits start to phase out, which would effectively reduce the tax penalties facing two earners (the current law already allows two-earner families to earn $1,000 more than single earners before the phaseout begins, and this break could be expanded). Or we could provide a three-year transition period during which individuals who get married would continue to be treated as individuals for EITC purposes.

Our preferred option is to disregard half of the lower-earning spouse's wages in computing the EITC in the phaseout range.[15] This plan increases costs by about $1 billion, but everyone who got married would either still get a subsidy from the tax system or face a penalty no larger than before (details are in the appendix to this chapter).[16] More broadly, it is possible to have different phaseout schedules for one- and two-parent families.

The total projected annual cost of this proposal is $9.8 billion. If limited to individuals age 21 to 45, it drops to $5.4 billion. Would the proposal significantly increase work effort? Our proposed subsidy is considerably larger than the New Hope subsidy, although it is smaller than the SSP subsidy or current EITC for individuals with children. All these programs have significantly increased participants' work effort. And the estimates of labor supply elasticities cited above (of 0.4–1.0; see references to Katz and Grogger above) suggest that a 20 percent increase in the real wages of low-wage workers should increase their employment rates by anywhere from 8 to 20 percent.

Given our proposal's cost, we also offer a more modest option. As observed in chapter 2 (and discussed more fully in chapter 6), work disincentives are a particular problem for low-wage noncustodial fathers who have large child support orders. One possibility would be to provide noncustodial fathers a special earned income credit if they are making their child support payments.[17] Specifically, we would make noncustodial fathers eligible for the current EITC, but we would cap the credit by the amount they are paying in child support. Our calculations suggest that, of the 1.16 million fathers who are currently paying child support and might be eligible for an expanded EITC, roughly 70 percent could receive an average of $1,600, at a net cost of about $1.2 billion.[18] The exact cost might well be higher, depending on the credit's take-up rate and how much it would actually change labor force and child support behavior among parents who work and pay little support; but the direct cost of these payments would not likely exceed $2 billion.

As with the expanded version of the EITC, this credit could create significant marriage penalties that would have to be addressed with a reduced phaseout for two-earner couples (which would add to the proposal's costs). A further criticism is that this scheme would help young men who have fathered children (and thus it might be seen as encouraging such behavior), while doing nothing to help the majority of young men who have not.

On the other hand, an expanded EITC would reward noncustodial parents who are supporting their children and should increase their child support payments as well as their work effort. Fathers would also likely become more involved with their children (Mincy 2002). And the larger social message would be that even young men who fathered children out of wedlock will be rewarded for "doing the right thing" and taking responsibility to work and support their children. The benefits of generating these changes seem to outweigh the credit's costs, at least in our opinion.

Our ideas are not particularly targeted on young workers—though our proposal to begin paying the credit at age 21 would ensure that older youth benefit from it. But, as we noted earlier, expectations of future earnings very likely affect young workers' employment and schooling decisions, so the expanded EITC could affect even those who are not currently eligible for it.

In sum, we propose three options for subsidies and tax credits:

- A wage subsidy for low-wage workers. The big advantage is that a subsidy would not create marriage penalties. The drawback is that it would not be targeted to low-income families and would be very expensive.
- An EITC of up to $1,500 for low-wage workers (including noncustodial parents), along with a provision mitigating the resulting marriage penalties. The annual cost would be $9.8 billion, unless the proposal is limited to 21- to 45-year-olds, in which case it falls to $5.4 billion.
- An EITC for low-wage noncustodial parents who are making their child support payments. The cost of this option is roughly $1 to $2 billion.

Our preference is for the second alternative, though we realize it may be difficult to enact in a time of tight budgets. At a minimum, we strongly support the third option. And, over the longer term, we would encourage that a wider range of benefits be made available to low-income workers, including health coverage, improved incentives for saving, and paid parental leave.[19]

Our proposals could be refined to be fairer, or less expensive, or possibly both. What matters is that something be done. Low-wage workers who are not on welfare and do not have custody of their children are the forgotten foot soldiers in the army of the poor, and low wages are their defining grievance. We now heavily subsidize low-income working custodial parents, but we do the opposite to noncustodial parents. But the problem is not limited to poor noncustodial parents. Millions of disadvantaged youth have little incentive to work in the above-ground economy because the wages they attract are so low. If we can improve their employment rates by subsidizing their wages, the benefits to their children, their communities, and the economy would make this modest public expense a wise investment.

NOTES

1. While the trends in labor force participation are not shown in table 5.1, they are quite similar to those that appear in table 5.2. A concern with these two tables is that the deterioration in the employment outcomes of less-educated men could reflect compositional changes in these groups as enrollment and schooling levels improve over time; these improvements imply that more-skilled high school students are attending college rather than entering the workforce. But this phenomenon should be even stronger for women than men, since college enrollment has increased more for the former; instead, the relative wages of less-educated women have improved compared to those of men.

2. The wider availability of Disability Insurance (DI) has also apparently led some less-educated men to drop out of the labor market. See Autor and Duggan (2003). Since the elderly have not been eliminated from this sample, earlier retirements among the less-educated might also contribute somewhat to the declining employment rates over time. But our estimates in which we limited the sample to those younger than 55 showed very similar results.

3. Most labor economists (e.g., Borjas 1996; Filer et al. 1996) suggest that work effort among prime-age men (25 to 54 years old) is not responsive to higher wages; in other words, their labor supply is quite inelastic, with work effort averaging roughly 40 hours per week regardless of net wages.

4. The target amount was $30,000 in New Brunswick in 1992 (it was higher in British Columbia), although this amount has been adjusted since then to reflect changes in the cost of living and in the amounts paid by the welfare system. See Michalopoulos and colleagues (2002).

5. Indeed, the EITC is by far the largest cash assistance program to the poor in the U.S. today. The federal government spends roughly twice as much on the EITC as it does on "welfare" through its block grant to the states under Temporary Assistance for Needy Families (TANF).

6. Some of these increases have been phased in over periods of 2 to 3 years. For example, the last increase in the federal minimum—from $4.25 to $5.15—was implemented partially in October 1996 and partially in October 1997.

7. Minorities constitute about 35 percent of those earning less than $8 per hour, while they are only about 23 percent of all workers (Chasanov 2004).

8. Higher minimum wages might also reduce employers' investments in training for young workers, since wages cannot temporarily be reduced to offset training costs. But how much on-the-job training minimum wage employers generate for their workers is questionable.

9. See Card and Krueger (1995) for a discussion of market imperfections in which higher minimum wages might raise, rather than lower, employment levels of youth. Also, see Holzer and LaLonde (2000) for evidence on young workers' turnover rates, and how

these are influenced by wage levels and other job characteristics as well as by personal characteristics.

10. In Phelps's scheme, the subsidy went to the employer rather than the worker. How much of the money ended up in workers' pockets and how much went to employers would depend on the elasticities of demand and supply.

11. The plan also contains administrative challenges: to determine who qualifies, each worker's hourly wage would have to be calculated, which is something the government does not do at the present.

12. President Reagan strongly supported the EITC, although some Republican members of Congress in recent years decried what they perceived as major fraud in the program.

13. Present law provides a small credit for such individuals, but it reaches a maximum at $382, and as such, it cannot possibly function as much of a work incentive for low-wage workers.

14. Currently those age 25 through 64 are eligible for the "childless EITC." We would not make those below age 21 eligible, as so many live with their parents or are still in school. At and above age 21, it might be possible administratively to eliminate eligibility for those enrolled in colleges or universities. On the other hand, some might argue that we should provide support for low-income students.

15. This is modeled on a plan proposed by Senator Tom Daschle (D-SD) in January 1999 (S. 8), which would have provided for a 20 percent deduction.

16. They might receive a smaller marriage subsidy, but we proceed here on the assumption that there is no public obligation to subsidize marriage, and reducing a marriage subsidy, whatever its shortcomings, is a reasonable price to pay for providing an increased work incentive to those who need it most.

17. One variant of this proposal would extend such credits to noncustodial fathers who are up-to-date on their child support payments—that is, they have no arrearages. We reject this approach because it would make most noncustodial fathers ineligible for the incentive.

18. We thank Elaine Sorensen for generating these estimates, using data for 2002 from the Urban Institute's National Survey of America's Families. Two offsets limit the new costs associated with expanding EITC payments: first, some noncustodial fathers already receive EITC payments because they are living with children from a new relationship; and second, others are receiving the current credit for childless individuals.

19. Economists would argue that universally provided public benefits could discourage work rather than encourage it. To avoid this problem, some benefits might be made available only to those who work (as they are in the case of paid parental leave); or, in the case of health benefits, be phased out much less quickly as income rises than they currently are under Medicaid.

Proposed Childless EITC

The Proposal

Under existing law, there is a small earned income tax credit for individuals without children and for noncustodial parents, equal to 7.65 percent of the first $5,000 of income. The credit remains unchanged between incomes of $5,000 and $6,260, after which it declines at a rate of 7.65 percent, phasing out at an income of about $11,200. The maximum credit is $383.

Under our proposal, this EITC would be increased to 20 percent of the first $7,500 of income, reaching a maximum of $1,500. Between incomes of $7,500 and $10,000, the credit would remain unchanged, after which it would decline by 15.98 percent for each dollar earned—the same phaseout rate as in the current program for households with one child.

Table 5.A.1 compares tax benefits resulting from the new proposal with benefits under current law.

Marriage Penalties

To address the problem of marriage penalties, we would add one additional feature to our proposal: a 50 percent discount in the phaseout range on the lower-earning spouse's wages. In other words, if one parent's earnings are $12,000 and the other's are $8,000, putting the family above the $13,730 phaseout, the second parent's earnings would be reduced to $4,000 for the purpose of calculating the EITC benefit.

How would our proposal affect marriage penalties and subsidies? To answer this question, we look at the typical four-person family (father, mother, and two children). We calculate marriage penalties or subsidies (1) under current law, (2) under current law with our basic proposal factored in, and (3) under current law with the proposal *and* the 50 percent discount provision.

We start by assuming that earnings are evenly split between the father and the mother because this, from the standpoint of marriage penalties, is the worst case. The results in table 5.A.2 show that when family income is

Table 5.A.1. *Proposed EITC for Noncustodial Parents, and Childless Individuals and Couples (dollars)*

Income	Credit under current law	Proposed new credit
1,000	77	200
2,000	153	400
3,000	230	600
4,000	306	800
5,000	383	1,000
6,000	383	1,200
7,000	383	1,400
8,000	326	1,500
9,000	249	1,500
10,000	173	1,500
11,000	96	1,340
12,000	20	1,180
13,000	0	1,021
14,000		861
15,000		701
16,000		541
17,000		381
18,000		222
19,000		62
20,000		0

Source: Urban Institute calculations using Urban Institute–Brookings Tax Policy Center data.

$5,000, and each earner makes $2,500, the net effect of all provisions in the tax code is a subsidy of $809. In other words, by being married, this couple is $809 better off than it would be if the two earners were living separately.[1] If total income is $15,000, the subsidy is $1,328, whereas if income is $30,000, the marriage penalty is $1,498.

The second column shows what happens when we add the new credit for childless people. Low-income couples are still better off married than single (at least from a tax standpoint), although the margin is smaller. At an income of $10,000, for instance, the marriage subsidy declines from $1,618 to $1,000. At an income of $20,000, however, whereas current law provides a marriage subsidy of $186, there is now a $1,218 penalty. And this same problem exists for incomes up to $40,000. However, penalties are mitigated by the 50 percent discount. Families with income

Table 5.A.2. *Marriage Penalties and Subsidies for a Four-Person Family with Earnings Split 50-50 between Two Earners (dollars)*

Income	Current penalty/ (subsidy)	Proposed penalty/ (subsidy)	Proposal plus 50% discount
5,000	(809)	(500)	(500)
10,000	(1,618)	(1,000)	(1,000)
15,000	(1,328)	(115)	(166)
20,000	(186)	1,218	165
25,000	437	1,537	221
30,000	1,498	2,199	620
35,000	2,353	2,655	1,410
40,000	2,417	2,417	2,299

Source: Urban Institute calculations using Urban Institute–Brookings Tax Policy Center data.

Note: The four-person family would include two adults and two children.

up to $15,000 are still better off married than single. At $20,000, the situation is essentially unchanged. Above that, the discount reduces marriage penalties at every income level.

Our analysis ignores the welfare system and its marriage penalties, which could well offset the tax system's subsidies. While we cannot fully discuss this topic here, we can provide some initial insights. When a low-income mother with children gets married, it is unlikely that earnings will be split 50-50 between the family's two adults. If we assume a more realistic 80-20 split, we get the numbers in table 5.A.3. Comparing column 3 with column 1, we see that, up to $25,000, marriage subsidies are somewhat lower than under current law, although they are still substantial. Between $25,000 and $35,000, however, marriage subsidies are larger.

Conclusion

If our analysis is limited to the federal income tax system, all low-income couples currently have an incentive to marry. The expanded EITC for noncustodial parents and childless individuals (along with the 50 percent discount) being proposed here would not change that. While our proposal would reduce marriage subsidies for some couples, it would

Table 5.A.3. *Marriage Penalties and Subsidies for a Four-Person Family with Earnings Split 80-20 between Two Earners (dollars)*

Earnings	Current penalty/ (subsidy)	Proposed penalty/ (subsidy)	Proposal plus 50% discount
5,000	(1,294)	(800)	(800)
10,000	(2,971)	(1,720)	(1,720)
15,000	(3,835)	(2,655)	(2,706)
20,000	(3,342)	(2,801)	(3,222)
25,000	(2,989)	(2,989)	(3,516)
30,000	(1,856)	(1,856)	(2,488)
35,000	(465)	(465)	(1,155)
40,000	165	165	165

Source: Urban Institute calculations using Urban Institute–Brookings Tax Policy Center data.

Note: The four-person family would include two adults and two children.

increase them for others, and it would reduce marriage penalties for many more. When combined with marriage penalties in the welfare system, marriage would be encouraged in some cases and discouraged in others. Where it is discouraged, the marriage disincentives would be relatively small in most cases, and they would be the result of welfare provisions unaffected by our proposal. Meanwhile, other families' marriage incentives would increase.

NOTES

All results presented in this appendix are based on simulations computed for us by Adam Carasso of the Urban Institute, using data from the Urban Institute–Brookings Tax Policy Center. We are grateful for his assistance.

1. We assume that, if the mother and father lived separately, both children would be with one of the adults.

6

Reconnecting Noncustodial Parents and Ex-Offenders

Two groups of young men face unusually strong disincentives and other barriers to work: noncustodial fathers and ex-offenders. These groups include many young African-American men below the age of 24 and even more black men in their late 20s and early 30s. Indeed, a quarter of less-educated black men between the ages of 16 and 24 are noncustodial fathers, as are roughly half of those age 25 to 34. And up to 30 percent of young African-American men have been incarcerated. Among whites and Hispanics, the incidence of previous incarceration is lower but still not trivial.

We focus somewhat less in this chapter on preventing youth involvement in crime and early fatherhood per se; these are major aims of the education and training programs we reviewed in chapters 3 and 4. Instead, we now look at the specific labor market problems faced by the many young men who have been incarcerated or become noncustodial fathers, as well as policy recommendations for dealing with these problems. We also look, more briefly, at steps to limit the participation of at-risk youth in crime, and alternatives to traditional youth criminal justice policies that might limit incarceration and recidivism.

Noncustodial Parents

From the standpoint of low-income noncustodial parents, the current child support system has at least four problems: (1) child support orders are unrealistically high and significantly reduce the incentive to work; (2) noncustodial parents see little reason to pay child support because almost none of the money ends up going to their children; (3) large arrearages tend to build up, further alienating noncustodial parents; and (4) little help is offered for noncustodial parents who cannot afford to pay child support. We deal with each of these in turn. As in the previous chapter, our policy recommendations are not explicitly aimed at youth, though young noncustodial fathers would likely be heavily influenced by their enactment.

Orders

Child support is a regressive system that places a greater burden on non-custodial parents at the bottom of the economic ladder than those further up. To some extent, this is unavoidable—child support is based on the costs of supporting children, and these costs consume a higher proportion of the poor's income. Still, the child support orders imposed on low-income parents frequently exceed their ability to pay, with serious consequences that deserve attention.

Roughly 3.5 million noncustodial parents are poor. Of these, about 1 million pay child support, even though their median annual earnings are only $5,000. One-quarter of these pay more than half their gross income in child support.[1] This likely represents a regressive transfer of resources—from the very poor to the less poor. In Maryland, for instance, if both the custodial parent and the noncustodial parent earn $10,000, and the latter is fully paying child support, the custodial parent ends up at 124 percent of the poverty level, while the noncustodial parent ends up at 58 percent.[2]

A related problem is that for low-wage noncustodial parents who pay child support, work incentives are all but eliminated. As total income rises from $5,000 to $15,000 in the states examined in table 6.1, disposable income (defined as total earnings minus federal and state taxes, work expenses, and child support, plus food stamps) barely increases. In California, for instance, noncustodial parents whose earnings increase from $5,000 to $15,000 see child support orders rise from $824 per year to $5,027; after other tax increases and losses of benefits are factored in, dis-

Table 6.1. *Disposable Income for Noncustodial Parents Making Child Support Payments*

State	Disposable Income ($) Starting from			Change in disposable income from $5,000 to $15,000 ($)	Marginal tax rate (%)
	$5,000	*$10,000*	*$15,000*		
Maryland	4,805	5,414	6,472	1,667	83.3
California	5,370	6,204	6,791	1,421	85.8
Texas	4,995	6,330	8,475	3,480	65.2

Source: Primus (2002a).

posable income rises from $5,370 to $6,791, an increase of $1,421.[3] So while earnings go up by $10,000, disposable income goes up by $1,421. This is equivalent to an 86 percent tax rate. While the example may be unusual, marginal tax rates of 20 to 35 percent due to child support alone are about average (Holzer et al. 2005), and total tax rates on average (including the effects of payroll taxes and lost eligibility for benefits) are no doubt much higher. On this basis, many low-income noncustodial parents likely decide they have little reason to work in the legitimate economy.[4]

To what extent do the "tax rates" associated with child support orders really drive low-income men out of the labor market? No one knows for sure, but the little we do know gives us pause.[5] As we noted above, Holzer and his colleagues (2005) found that the more vigorous child support enforcement of the 1990s (as well as rising numbers of men with criminal records) depressed employment and labor force activity among young black men, even as the economy experienced its strongest expansion period since the end of World War II. The estimated effects were stronger among men age 25 to 34 than among men age 16 to 24, which makes sense (given the greater incidence of noncustodial fatherhood in the former age group). Three steps, not mutually exclusive, can be taken to help:

- We can encourage states to revise their guidelines to reflect the circumstances of low-wage noncustodial parents. For instance, the federal government could fund a national commission or state commissions to investigate all aspects of child support, including orders for low-wage men.

- Congress could limit the orders imposed on low-wage noncustodial parents. For instance, a noncustodial parent earning less than $5,000 while supporting one child would pay no more than 5 percent of income in child support; between $5,000 and $10,000, the maximum would be 15 percent; between $10,000 and $20,000, it would be 23 percent, as illustrated below. The argument against federal limits is that child support guidelines are a state matter. There would undoubtedly be an outcry if the federal government limited orders. On the other hand, the states are unlikely to reform their child support systems on their own.
- As proposed in chapter 5, we could provide a credit to low-wage non-custodial parents who are making their child support payments.

Overall, we strongly support the first and third options and believe that the second should be considered as well.

Pass-Through

Before 1996, in child support cases involving families on welfare, states were only required to pass $50 a month of collected support payments to the custodial parent. But the welfare reform law of 1996 eliminated even this requirement. Since then, states have had the option of forwarding child support collections to the custodial parent, but at the states' own expense (in other words, the federal government does nothing to offset the loss of revenues to states that pass child support through to custodial parents). Not surprisingly, few states have exercised this option; low-income noncustodial parents now argue that, apart from the fear of sanctions, they have little incentive to pay child support because it goes into state coffers rather than to their children.

Table 6.2. *Potential Federal Caps on Child Support Orders for Low-Income Parents*

Earnings ($)	One child (% of income)	Two children (% of income)
0–5,000	5	5
5,000–10,000	15	25
10,000–20,000	23	35

Source: Authors' calculations.

Little reliable research exists on whether collections would increase if passed on to the custodial family. Recently, however, the State of Wisconsin received federal permission to implement such a policy, and while the program is still relatively young, early indications are promising. A report from the Institute for Research on Poverty at the University of Wisconsin finds that, when custodial mothers received the entire child support payment, paternity was more likely to be established and child support to be paid—and in larger amounts.[6]

Before the federal welfare changes of 1996, one of the arguments against passing through child support collections was that it encouraged women to stay on welfare indefinitely. With current time limits on welfare receipt, however, that argument no longer applies. Helping mothers leave the welfare rolls and get out of poverty is an excellent policy goal, and passing through child support collections clearly contributes to that goal.

Arrearages

Arrearages, the amounts past due in child support, now exceed $80 billion.[7] In 1999, 82 percent of Maryland fathers who owed child support had arrearages; the average amount owed was $6,834. The comparable figures for Oregon were 84 percent and $6,301.[8] Arrearages of this size have a demoralizing effect on noncustodial parents because most of them have little hope of paying them off. In addition, states can (and often do) garnish up to 65 percent of earnings while noncustodial parents are in arrears, thus creating very high marginal tax rates on earnings. Noncustodial parents with large arrearages identify them as a key deterrent to paying child support.[9] Better to get a job off the books or in the underground, where the authorities won't be able to track them down.

In addressing arrearages, the first step is to reform the process of establishing orders. Normally, if a noncustodial father does not show up at the hearing or cannot produce reliable information on earnings, the court will assume that he is able to earn a certain income. Sometimes, support payments are calculated back to the time the child was born, even if no action was taken to establish paternity until much later. Or the noncustodial father may be required to pay for the child's delivery, likely several thousand dollars. If the noncustodial father does not show up at the hearing, the result is a default order which may be wholly unrealistic in its assumptions about his ability to pay. Default orders are common—in Los Angeles County, for instance, default orders were set in 79 percent of all cases in 2002. Los Angeles is a worst-case example, but even in Connecticut default orders were set in 20 percent of all support cases.[10]

Default orders are a necessary part of the judicial process, and justified when a parent knowingly fails to respond to court action. This is not always the case, however. Noncustodial fathers may not show up because they never received the order to appear (low-income people are often transient), or they may not understand the order because of language difficulties or literacy problems. In any event, reducing the number of default orders—by making greater effort to locate low-income noncustodial parents or to learn about their economic circumstances—should be a top priority. When orders are set by default, they are likely to be based on unrealistic assumptions and arrearages will pile up. That is a recipe for trouble.

Second, states should make it easier to amend orders when incomes change. When a low-income father is incarcerated, for instance, pretending that he can continue paying child support makes little sense. The same is true of unemployment. In most states, though, amending a child support order is no simple matter. Furthermore, most low-income fathers do not know how to navigate the system, and are in no position to pay for an attorney who can do it for them.

Before 1996, states had to review child support orders every three years for parents receiving welfare; otherwise, orders were reviewed at the request of either parent. Now, however, mandatory reviews are no longer required, and parents not on welfare who request a review outside the regular three-year cycle must demonstrate a "substantial change in circumstances," which many are unable to do.[11] So the revision of unrealistic and outdated support orders is even more of a problem.

Third, states should be encouraged to develop arrearage amnesty programs to encourage noncustodial parents to participate in the child support system. A few states are already doing this. In effect, some portion of the arrearage is forgiven if the noncustodial father consistently makes his child support payments. There are limits to such schemes: states can only forgive money owed to the state, not money owed to the family. Still, such arrangements make sense: the state loses little—it is not likely to collect the arrearage anyway—and the noncustodial father gets a second chance to fulfill his paternal duties without an 800-pound boulder hanging around his neck.[12]

Helping Low-Income Noncustodial Parents Improve their Earnings

Not surprisingly, many low-income fathers have trouble meeting their child support obligations. Most of their problems are with employment and closely related to the disconnection we have discussed in this book. For instance, over 40 percent of low-income noncustodial parents are high school dropouts, whose employment rates have been declining for over thirty years. Over one-third are black men. At any given time, only half of poor noncustodial fathers are working.[13]

Low-income men need employment services similar to those provided to low-income women as part of the last decade's welfare reform effort. The 1996 law opened the door to this possibility—states were permitted to use their TANF dollars to help low-income men obtain job training and to assist them with other employment activities—but no special funding was provided for this purpose; as a result, little progress has been made. Today, almost all of the TANF dollars allocated to employment services go to help custodial mothers. As part of the Balanced Budget Act of 1997, Congress also authorized $3 billion in welfare-to-work grants that could be used to serve noncustodial parents, but these funds, too, went largely to serve custodial parents. Little was left for noncustodial parents.

The one past effort to help noncustodial men that has been rigorously evaluated is the Parents' Fair Share (PFS) initiative, an outgrowth of the Family Support Act of 1988. Aimed at low-income noncustodial fathers who owed child support for children who were on welfare, PFS provided employment, training, and support services with the goals of increasing employment, income, child support payments, and parental involvement. More than 5,000 noncustodial fathers in seven locations across the country were randomly assigned to an experimental or control group and studied over two years. The child-support obligations of the experimental group were reduced while they were in the program, but obligations were also more strictly enforced.

The major finding of the PFS evaluation, conducted by the Manpower Demonstration Research Corporation (MDRC), was that child support payments increased modestly. This occurred largely because of the smoke-out effect—some of the men referred to the program were forced to acknowledge that they were already working. The program did not increase employment, however, and incorporated relatively little skill-building because program participants had no way of supporting themselves while they were in training.[14]

The other major problem identified in the evaluation was that PFS had no way to assist participants who were unsuccessful in finding work. PFS would enroll participants in job search training, but if they did not find a job within three to six months, they were free to stop looking. The program was mandatory in name only, the critics charged.

Two conclusions follow:

- A program for noncustodial fathers must include public jobs so that participants who do not find private employment can still work to help support their families (as recommended by MDRC).
- If job training is to be provided, the program must pay stipends. Otherwise, enrollments will be minimal, and most participants will enroll in job search training with the program having little lasting impact, as was true of Parents' Fair Share. Noncustodial parents' incentives to participate might also be improved through some additional "carrots," such as access to Medicaid for those paying child support.

The bottom line is that we need a dedicated funding stream covering employment services for low-income noncustodial fathers. The effort is likely to be expensive, but the U.S. is currently spending billions on TANF, not to mention state and other federal dollars, to help welfare mothers find jobs and make the transition to the world of work. We now need to do something similar for the men.

On the other hand, because a great deal of uncertainty remains about exactly how to help disadvantaged men, we should begin with some rigorously evaluated demonstration projects. Primus (2002b) has outlined some intriguing possibilities that provide strong incentives for noncustodial parents to participate and impose reciprocal obligations on them in return for benefits. In some cases, employment services for fathers would be combined with family counseling, perhaps even encouraging marriage among young parents; in other cases, services would be an explicit part of a package of obligations for young offenders as conditions for their parole or probation. In all cases, noncustodial fathers would have access to employment and training services along with cash stipends and health care benefits to encourage their participation.

Recommendations for Policy

For most of the last thirty years, the child support movement has focused on stricter enforcement and more vigorous prosecution. On the whole, we support this trend and believe it has benefited families with children. The problem is that, in all the give-and-take of the struggle to improve enforcement, low-income fathers were forgotten. We need to make sure that child support awards are set reasonably, that incentives to work are preserved, and that large arrearages are avoided whenever possible—in short, we do not want to drive these men out of the mainstream job market into the underground economy.

This will require a total change in the way the child support system treats low-income fathers. The system is already changing in a few places but must change everywhere. The problems affecting noncustodial parents have built up over many years and are closely connected, involving employment, family relations, and a host of other factors. To be effective, the response will have to be equally comprehensive and coordinated.

Our specific recommendations are summarized as follows:

- *We need to change how orders are set and updated for low-income men.* Both the House-passed and Senate Finance Committee–reported TANF reauthorization bills pending as of spring 2005 require states to review orders for parents on TANF every three years, but this is just one step. The bigger challenge is finding ways to reduce default orders, retroactive awards, and the imputation of income, and to address orders set at levels beyond noncustodial parents' ability to pay. And we need to convince more states to test arrearage forgiveness schemes that reward noncustodial parents who cooperate with the system.
- *We recommend that states pass through as much child support as possible to families who are on welfare (or have left welfare).* One important question is whether the federal government will share in the cost of passing through child support. The TANF reauthorization bill passed by the House in early 2005 provides for a limited pass-through. The version approved by the Senate Finance Committee in spring 2005 (but not by the full Senate as of this writing) included a much broader provision.[15] The Senate version is far preferable.
- *Greater efforts need to be made to improve noncustodial parents' earnings capacity.* But given mixed findings from the Parents' Fair Share evaluation, it makes sense to proceed cautiously. While welfare

reform has successfully reduced caseloads over the last eight years, no one knows whether a similar approach will work for low-income men. Accordingly, we recommend a series of demonstration projects that build on Parents' Fair Share. We need to go through the same experimentation and evaluation for noncustodial fathers that we did for welfare mothers in the eighties and nineties.

Such changes won't be easy. Child support policy decisions are almost all made by the states, with the emphasis on increasing support collections, not helping low-income men. In part, of course, this is because the states have responded accordingly to federal government rewards for increasing collections. There is no reason why the incentives cannot be changed to reflect new priorities. Change will require a major effort, though. Low-income men are hardly a favored constituency in state capitols (or in congressional hearing rooms, for that matter). By contrast, groups representing custodial parents and poor women generally have considerable sway, and they are not much interested in the marginal tax rates on low-income men. In congressional testimony, a few feminist groups have opposed employment services for noncustodial fathers, even though one of the main goals was to increase child support payments.

So change will be difficult, and it will be slow, and in the end it will only come if Congress insists on it. But, as we have argued, the social benefits potentially generated by higher employment among young noncustodial fathers are worth the effort.

Young Offenders

Another group of youth who are disconnected from the labor market and the educational system are those with criminal records, especially those who have been incarcerated in either a juvenile or adult facility.

The number of people incarcerated in the U.S. is extraordinary—roughly 2 million currently in local jails or state and federal prisons, about 90 percent of whom are men and roughly two-thirds of whom are black or Hispanic. Most are not serving life sentences—in fact, the average length of stay in prison is roughly three years—so about a third (or about 650,000) are released from prison or jail each year (Travis et al. 2001). Of these, approximately 200,000 are 24 or younger, and about 100,000 are still teens. Freeman (2003) has estimated that about 7 percent of the adult male noninstitutional population in the U.S. has been incarcerated; but among young black men, a comparable rate would be closer to 30 percent.[16] About one-third of young black men will have served time before they reach age 35.

Widespread incarceration might well reduce crime rates in the U.S., especially in the absence of other methods of crime prevention (e.g., Levitt 2004). But its negative impacts on young men have become clearer over time. Ex-offenders have worse outcomes in the labor market than most other groups of disadvantaged people; their earnings and employment rates are low, even relative to others with similar skills and backgrounds (Freeman 1992; Western, Kling, and Weiman 2001). Of course, poor skills and limited work experience, poor physical and mental health, racial discrimination, and residence in poor neighborhoods with few nearby employment opportunities and weak informal networks all contribute to ex-offenders' difficulties, and would even had they not been incarcerated. But time spent in prison further erodes any skills, experience, or labor market contacts ex-offenders might have once had, while their trust in and attachment to mainstream institutions and modes of behavior weaken. Even for ex-offenders who become employed, retention rates are very low over a six-month period and beyond (Bushway 2003).

On the demand side of the labor market, employers are wary of hiring young men with criminal records. Holzer, Raphael, and Stoll (2004) show that employers are more averse to hiring from this group than from virtually any other, including welfare mothers and those with little recent work experience. In fact, employers would only consider filling about 40 percent of recent noncollege job openings with otherwise qualified ex-offenders, but would consider filling 80 to 90 percent of these job openings with welfare recipients and others with little recent employment.

Employers fear legal liabilities if offenders steal from or harm customers or coworkers—and they fear being harmed themselves. State and federal laws frequently bar employers from hiring offenders in growing sectors of the economy—especially those involving child care, elder care, health care, and financial services. In fact, some of the economic sectors and occupations where ex-offenders are most employable, such as unskilled manufacturing, are shrinking as percentages of the workforce. Where jobs are available to those with criminal records, wages are often near the minimum and benefits or job security virtually nonexistent.

Of course, employers are not always aware of exactly who is or is not an ex-offender; while many employers ask this information on their applications, there is no particular reason to believe the answers are truthful.

About 60 percent of employers now check criminal records when filling jobs that do not require a college education—a figure that has risen in recent years, as searches have become easier through online services. But questions remain about the accuracy of online background checks, especially those from unregulated private companies (Bushway et al. 2004). For example, some apparently use arrest rather than conviction records.[17]

And the stigma associated with a criminal record clearly varies by race. In an audit study of hiring in Milwaukee, Pager (2003) found employers reluctant to make offers to young blacks and to young men with criminal records, but especially to young black men with criminal records. Pairs of white and black men with identical levels of education (high school diploma) and work experience, one admitting to a criminal record while one did not, were sent on job interviews. Of whites who were not ex-offenders, 34 percent received callbacks from employers while only 14 percent of blacks did; among offenders, the comparable fractions were 17 percent and 4 percent.

Thus, most studies show very modest employment rates among recently released offenders.[18] In addition, ex-offenders face a range of difficulties besides getting or keeping jobs. Finding housing and getting health services are major challenges, especially for those with HIV or substance abuse problems. Even getting basic legal identification is often difficult, as many states deny drivers' licenses to those with criminal convictions. And federal law compounds these difficulties in many ways—for instance, those with drug convictions are barred from public housing, Pell Grants, and other benefits (like TANF or food stamps).

For young offenders, the basic demographics are no more encouraging than for the population of ex-offenders as a whole. The vast majority lack high school diplomas, at least partly due to their young ages (about 30 percent of those released are age 17 or less); most are also functionally illiterate, with 60 percent reading at or below the 6th-grade level. About two-thirds are habitual drug users; at least two-thirds and perhaps as many as 80 percent suffer from mental health or learning disabilities such as attention deficit disorder, anxiety or mood disorders, and depression. HIV and other infections (such as hepatitis C) are common as well (Altschuler and Brash 2003; Snyder 2003).

But these problems, which are common to ex-offenders of all ages, are intensified for young offenders. For instance, most young offenders expect to live with family members upon release. But their relationships with family and friends are often strained by their participation in crime, and frequently their families are poor and unstable. Thus, ex-offenders are not always able to resume residence with their immediate families. They may also find returning to school unappealing, since many have dropped out or been expelled for their behavior. Most schools are not anxious for young offenders to return, and most offenders show little interest in returning to schools where they previously failed and where they now might be years older than their classmates.

Many scholars (e.g., Steinberg, Chung, and Little 2003) argue that young offenders suffer from poor psychosocial development magnified by their incarceration. Removing young offenders from their homes and families, as well as confining them with other offenders who have all failed in a variety of ways, may well exacerbate developmental deficits that existed prior to incarceration. Returning young offenders are thus out-of-sync with their chronological counterparts as well as their families, and frequently gravitate to peers on the street, especially in poor neighborhoods with very few appealing employment options (Sullivan 2003). Not surprisingly, recidivism rates among young offenders are very high, in the range of 55 to 75 percent within three years (Travis and Visher, forthcoming).

Furthermore, young offenders are often less stable and mature, and less motivated to make positive changes than are at least some of their older counterparts. Programs that have shown some success at improving employment outcomes or reducing recidivism among older male offenders seem less successful with this population. For instance, Uggen's (2000) reanalysis of data from the Supported Work experiment of the 1970s shows significantly positive impacts on earnings and employment for male ex-offenders older than 26, but no effects for younger men.[19] Little is known about mapping successful life trajectories for young offenders (Travis and Visher, forthcoming).

The difficulties associated with young offenders' characteristics and behaviors are exacerbated by the institutions in which they are incarcerated, as well as recent policy changes. Juvenile institutions are frequently overcrowded, poorly supervised, and violent (Cannon 2004). Moreover, as a consequence of the "get tough" policies of the 1990s, juveniles are increasingly likely to be incarcerated in adult facilities. Overall, a rising incarcerated population, along with less-rapidly rising correctional budgets, has reduced funding for substance abuse treatment or education within prisons. Indeed, only 13 percent of released offenders had been through prerelease planning, and under 10 percent had been treated for substance abuse problems (Travis and Visher, forthcoming). Only one-third received any educational instruction, and only about one-fourth received any type of vocational training.

The relationship (or lack thereof) between correctional institutions and other potential service providers also makes it less likely that young offenders will be well-served after release. Schools, health care and job training services, and community organizations are generally fragmented and disconnected from the corrections systems. For one thing, prisons are physically segregated from communities, so their location alone limits cooperation among social services. Furthermore, most other service providers focus on a single type of service rather than on meeting a wide range of needs; and their missions and outlook differ considerably from that of correctional institutions. No single entity is responsible for tracking young offenders after their release or providing them with services. As we noted above, many school systems have incentives (probably strengthened under No Child Left Behind) to avoid young offenders who may drain their attention and resources, and would reduce average scores on statewide tests.

And young men's incentives to seek help and reengage in school or work are slim, given their previous failures. Also, since large fractions of young offenders are also noncustodial fathers who have gone into arrears while incarcerated (if not earlier), the child support obligation often heightens the disincentives.

Some Options and Promising Models

Despite the daunting set of challenges we face in helping young offenders reenter the worlds of school and work, at least some ideas have been formulated and some models developed that seem worth supporting and pursuing further.

Some of these models focus on efforts that occur *prerelease,* while the young men remain incarcerated. These models focus on

- education and training;
- work experience; and
- prerelease planning.

The effectiveness of education and training for the incarcerated has been challenged (Bushway 2003), and little separate evaluation evidence exists for young, as opposed to adult, offenders. Given the generally weak labor market returns for GEDs (e.g., Cameron and Heckman 1993) and more recent evidence that their positive impacts for ex-offenders are short-lived (Tyler and Kling 2004), investing heavily in GED attainment is probably not the most effective use of the limited resources available for offenders.[20] Wherever possible, opportunities for young offenders to earn real high school diplomas probably deserve support. On the other hand, some positive impacts have been found in a random-assignment evaluation of the North Carolina Vocational Delivery System, which provided both training and employment services for young men (Lattimore, Witte, and Baker 1990). Not surprisingly, the training's effectiveness seems to depend on its timing—shortly before release works best—and relevance to existing jobs and employers who are willing to hire offenders upon release (Cullen and Gendreau 2000).

The positive effects of in-prison work experience on postrelease employment have been clearly noted in the research literature (e.g., Saylor and Gaes 1996), and these seem to be confirmed in a more recent analysis by economist Jeffrey Kling of Princeton and his colleagues.[21] But, while some inmates are involved in jobs that provide services for their institutions (such as laundry, janitorial work, or food services), very few are engaged in work for pay, such as provided by Federal Prison Industries or the private sector (Atkinson and Rostad 2003).[22] Currently, opportunities for employment are limited by federal regulations, and some efforts in Congress would further restrict them.[23] Expanding the options for real work experience among inmates on work release or even while fully incarcerated is controversial politically, but could have positive effects on employment outcomes after incarceration.

Whatever schooling, training, or work experience is generated for young offenders while they are incarcerated, the need for better planning before their release seems critical. Family members and community organizations need to be more fully and regularly involved in prerelease planning, so that services and support can be provided at this critical moment. Some positive examples of prerelease planning with inmates and their families can be found in the Florida Department of Corrections Office of Citizens' Services, which seeks to improve communication between inmates' families and the justice system. Also, a private nonprofit community group on Manhattan's lower east side, La Bodega de la Familia, provides drug abuse treatment and prevention services in which families of drug offenders participate. Services include case management, support groups, and a 24-hour hotline for emergencies. Opened in 1996, La

Bodega de la Familia is operated by the Vera Institute of Justice with financial support from the City of New York and serves about 40 families at any given time. Though La Bodega de la Familia has not been rigorously evaluated, data show substantial declines in drug use, criminal involvement, and recidivism among program participants relative to a comparison group. Participants report greater family support and reduced drug arrests, as well. (Sullivan et al. 2002).

Regarding *postrelease* services and supports, the links between criminal justice systems and other community institutions or service providers were recently analyzed in the Youth Offender Demonstration Project run by the U.S. Department of Labor from 1999 to 2001. The Youth Offender demonstration, run at 14 sites around the country, mostly sought to improve coordination across institutions and service providers for young offenders in various communities. The demonstration's process evaluation (Research and Evaluation Associates 2002) generally found that the links it encouraged among courts, probation officers, community organizations, and service providers were fairly successful, but those involving local school systems and employers were much more problematic. Improving schools' and employers' incentives to deal with young offenders, perhaps by improving the services offered to the offenders themselves, remains a major challenge.

What other models of postrelease educational or employment services look promising? Some examples might include

- "aftercare" such as the Intensive Aftercare Program (IAP) or programs run by the Friends of the Island Academy in New York;
- charter schools that focus predominantly on young offenders, such as the Community Prep program run by the Center for Alternative Sentencing and Employment Strategies (CASES) or the John V. Lindsay Wildcat Charter School in New York;
- programs run by labor market intermediaries and focusing on ex-offenders, such as the Center for Employment Opportunities (CEO) in New York or the Safer Foundation in Chicago, that help prepare offenders for the workforce and place them into jobs;
- "transitional jobs"—subsidized jobs in the private or nonprofit sector—that last up to 6 months before ex-offenders are placed in unsubsidized positions;
- other employment and training programs like the Job Corps and the Service Corps, which have proven track records for improving

high-risk youths' earnings and reducing crime and incarceration rates; and

- broader preventive efforts involving the criminal justice systems, schools, and community groups that deal with at-risk youth prior to incarceration (or reincarceration).

The IAP was developed in the late 1990s by David Altschuler of Johns Hopkins University and his colleagues, based on a federally funded multi-year study of best practices for reentry of juvenile offenders into their communities. The underlying theory is that reentry programs do not work as single programs but require broader systems and multiagency cooperation. The model provides intensive case management and a structured, gradual transition into schooling or employment after release from incarceration (Juvenile Reintegration and Aftercare Center 2004). The program is currently in operation at three sites (Denver, Las Vegas, and Norfolk, Virginia) and is being evaluated using random assignment methods by the National Council on Crime and Delinquency (Wiebush, McNulty, and Le 2000).

The programs run by Friends of the Island Academy (the "Island" refers to Rikers Island) are based on a holistic model that provides a comprehensive range of services to young current and former inmates in New York. The services include basic education (leading to the GED), mentoring, education in life-management skills, employment preparation and job placement, substance abuse treatment, and individualized case management. Created in 1990 to address a recidivism rate of over 70 percent, the program currently serves about 500 former young offenders at any time and offers prevention programs to thousands of at-risk youth. In 2004, 59 percent of postrelease participants were African-American and 31 percent were Hispanic; 89 percent were men. The reincarceration rate of participants in 2003–2004 was 5 percent.

The Community Prep High School run by CASES and the John V. Lindsay Wildcat Charter School (formerly the Wildcat Academy) are charter schools designed primarily for reentering young offenders. CASES operates a dozen direct-service programs for youth and adult offenders that reach nearly 14,000 people annually. Community Prep is designed to help youth move between the juvenile justice system and traditional high schools, GED completion, or employment. Foundation-funded, it emphasizes literacy and includes counseling, tutoring, and after-school programs (Rimer 2004).

Wildcat, in particular, shares characteristics of high school reform we identified in chapter 3—namely, small class sizes, sustained relationships with caring adults, opportunities for employment, and a culture emphasizing self-discipline and respect (Betanzos 2003). Students alternate between taking classes for a week and then working at internships for a week. The school also maintains ties with prosecutors, probation officers, and local police as part of its attempts to prevent relapses into crime and reincarceration; and it maintains close ties with mental health and other service providers, referring students for treatment whenever necessary. Founded in 1992, Wildcat now operates year-round at two locations, one in Manhattan and one in the Bronx. In 2004, 76 percent of the graduating class of the Manhattan school went to college. The school is affiliated with the Wildcat Service Corporation, which since 1972 has been imparting hard and soft employment skills to more than 8,500 former offenders a year.

CEO and the Safer Foundation focus primarily on adult offenders and youth who want to reenter the labor market. CEO serves 1,800 released offenders each year, providing job preparation skills and job development assistance through its Vocational Development Program. Counselors meet with participants to help them develop an employment plan, arrange job interviews, and provide ongoing support after placement, including communication with employers. Each participant also gets a temporary paid job in CEO's Neighborhood Work Project, often in the food service or nonprofit sectors, for three to six months; jobs typically develop into permanent positions. CEO's job-readiness training includes sessions on resume writing, job search, interview preparation, and discussing a criminal record with a potential employer (Buck 2000). CEO is one of seven workforce development organizations participating in a rigorous evaluation of programs for the "hard to serve." Selected randomly, experimental group participants will receive all of CEO's services, while control group members will have access only to CEO's career resource center.

The Safer Foundation, founded in 1972, does not provide transitional jobs but a range of services that include education, training, and job placement assistance. Safer works closely with participants to prepare them for workplace culture and provides postemployment counseling and assistance with workplace problems. It also advises employers on tax benefits for hiring ex-offenders. With programs across Illinois and Iowa, Safer also runs some in-prison educational programs in the Cook County jail and a work-release center.

CEO and Safer have each worked by now with several hundred local employers, and each pays close attention to employers' needs for job-ready and productive employees. Each also provides postplacement support services in an attempt to reduce clients' high job turnover rates.

Transitional jobs programs have now been run for ex-offenders and other hard-to-employ people in several major cities (Kirby et al. 2002). Similar in some ways to the Supported Work model of the 1970s, transitional jobs programs provide temporary employment in a nonprofit setting along with a range of supports and services. Each employee is paid at least the minimum wage and is usually eligible for the EITC and other benefits. Employment is explicitly viewed as part of a transition to what ideally will be stable private-sector work. Program costs, including both wages and support services, are generally $1,000 to $2,000 per month for each participant.

The Job Corps and the Youth Service Corps, described at length in chapter 3, both have a demonstrated ability not only to improve earnings but also to reduce arrests (and rearrests) for at-risk youth. In random assignment evaluations, the Service Corps reduced arrests by nearly a third (from 17 percent to 12 percent in the 15-month follow-up period; see Jastrzab et al. 1997) while Job Corps reduced arrests by less in proportional terms (from 30 percent to 25 percent) but over a longer period (30 months; see Ivry and Doolittle 2003).

Finally, a range of broader efforts to prevent first-time incarceration or recidivism among offenders has been outlined by Katzmann (2002). He envisions a range of local partnerships involving criminal justice officials (including police and probation officers), the legal system (including prosecutors, defense attorneys, and judges), schools, mental health service providers, the child welfare system, government agencies, and community groups. Partnerships would be designed to identify individuals at risk of incarceration and treat the various sources of their behavioral problems. A range of current local examples is provided, such as the Ten Point Coalition and the Gun Project in Boston (where the religious community acted as intermediaries between the police and local gangs); the Safety First project in Lowell, Massachusetts (a partnership of criminal justice officials, city agencies, and community groups); and partnerships between local police units and mental health providers in New Haven, Connecticut, and Boston. In many ways, the partnerships Katzmann envisions and describes resemble the community systems we described in chapter 4, though Katzmann focuses primarily on crime prevention and rehabilitation rather than education and employment.

The Ten Point Coalition is a faith-based group founded in 1992 in response to a gang-related shooting and stabbing during a funeral for a murder victim. Ten Point has 52 clergy and lay members whose purpose is to reduce violence and drug abuse among high-risk youth. Its ten points are (1) adopting youth gangs; (2) sending mediators and mentors into courts, schools, juvenile detention facilities, and the streets; (3) assigning youth workers to intervene with drug dealers and gang leaders on the streets; (4) developing concrete alternatives to the drug economy; (5) linking downtown and suburban churches to inner-city churches; (6) instituting neighborhood crime watches; (7) developing partnerships with community health centers; (8) establishing brotherhoods and sisterhoods as alternatives to gang life; (9) establishing rape crisis centers, services for battered women, and counseling for abusive men; and (10) developing a curriculum to curb violence, build literacy, and enhance self-esteem in the black and Hispanic communities. While not the sole actor, the Ten Point Coalition helped in the remarkable achievement that no one under the age of 17 was murdered in Boston between 1995 and 1998 (Berrien and Winship 2003).

The Boston Gun Project is a partnership of area and federal law enforcement agencies and academic experts that began in 1995 to apply problem-solving theory to homicide reduction. The Gun Project inaugurated "Operation Ceasefire," an interagency working group that used systematic research techniques to study the dynamics of youth violence in Boston, developed interventions to reduce youth homicides, and evaluated their results. A Kennedy School of Government evaluation found that Operation Ceasefire was associated with significant reductions in youth homicide and gun assaults (Braga and Kennedy 2002; Kennedy 2002).

Unfortunately, very few of the programs discussed in this chapter (except for the Job Corps and the Youth Service Corps) have been rigorously evaluated to discover their impacts relative to their costs. Some programs are currently under evaluation, while others will continue to provide only encouraging data on program outcomes. Yet, given the massive costs imposed not only on the poor but on the U.S. as a whole by high crime rates and mass incarceration, there remains an enormous need to invest public resources in programs for young offenders while we continue to learn which are most effective.[24] The Bush administration's new initiative on prisoner reentry for fiscal year 2005, which would provide $300 million over the next four years to a variety of efforts (especially those that are "faith based"), is at least a start, but must be expanded with more resources and effort.

Policy Recommendations

In response to the challenge of reconnecting young offenders, we recommend

- expanding opportunities for education, training, and work experience for offenders while incarcerated;
- greater funding for prisoner reentry efforts at all levels of government, but with some funds explicitly set aside for programs dealing with young offenders;
- more funds for programs like Job Corps and Service Corps with proven records of success;
- a more aggressive agenda for rigorous evaluations of existing school, employment, and aftercare programs for young offenders; and
- more support for efforts to build institutional links (or "systems") that encompass criminal justice and parole officers, community organizations, service providers, schools, and employers.

These recommendations parallel those we offered for education and training in chapter 3; they are, in truth, a special subset of those recommendations. Young offenders suffer from many of the same problems as other disadvantaged and disconnected youth, albeit in more extreme form. On the other hand, given the severity of young offenders' problems and the large numbers of youth who now fall into this category, some targeting of funds and services seems appropriate as well.

NOTES

1. See Sorenson and Oliver (2002).
2. See Primus (2002a).
3. The availability of food stamps for individuals earning $5,000 per year enables their disposable income to be close to or above $5,000, despite child support orders and other taxes. Losing eligibility for food stamps as income rises contributes importantly to the high marginal tax rates on earnings that noncustodial fathers face.
4. If child support orders on low-income men are adjusted infrequently when their earnings rise, the example discussed above may be less relevant. On the other hand,

high implicit taxes on their earnings likely deter them from entering the formal labor market in the first place.

5. The effects of taxes on work effort, just like the effects of earnings supplements (such as the EITC) we discussed in chapter 5, depend on the "elasticity of labor supply" of the workers being taxed. In theory, the effect of taxes on work effort could be positive, negative, or zero; but the evidence cited in the earlier chapter suggests that the work effort for low-income men is positively correlated with their after-tax earnings, or negatively correlated with tax rates.

6. Meyer and Cancian (2001).

7. Sorenson and Oliver (2002).

8. See Primus (2002b).

9. See Waller and Plotnick (1999).

10. See Legler (2003).

11. Primus (2002a).

12. Of course, great care must be taken to ensure that amnesty programs do not create incentives to accumulate arrearages. In addition, amnesty must not be used to benefit noncustodial parents who have the ability to pay their child support and have simply refused to do so.

13. Sorenson and Oliver (2002).

14. Knox and Miller (2001).

15. See Turetsky (2003).

16. Freeman estimates that 22 percent of all black men have been incarcerated, and it is very likely that these rates are even higher for men in their twenties and thirties, who have been most heavily impacted by rising incarceration rates during the previous decade.

17. On the other hand, Holzer and his colleagues (2004) show that when employers check records, they engage in less statistical discrimination against black men—they are less likely to assume that black male job applicants might have criminal records after doing background checks and finding no records.

18. Several studies, including Pettit and Lyons (2004) and Tyler and Kling (2004), show that only 30 to 40 percent of ex-offenders have any employment in a given quarter. Of course, these figures—based on Unemployment Insurance wage records—omit more casual employment, and thus self-reported employment rates of ex-offenders (e.g., Freeman 1992) are much higher. But, even in studies that rely on the latter, offenders' employment rates lag behind those of comparably unskilled young men without criminal records.

19. The Supported Work program provided several months of intensive services and support in a nonprofit workplace for welfare recipients, ex-offenders, and other disadvantaged groups. The program was evaluated using random assignment techniques. Postprogram impacts on welfare recipients' earnings were very positive (Eberwein, Ham, and LaLonde 1997), though few positive effects were found at that time for other groups.

20. To the extent that GEDs are sometimes a stepping-stone to other postsecondary schooling, their estimated impacts on postincarceration employment and earnings may understate their positive impacts.

21. This research, based on the administrative files of the entire prison population in Florida, is currently in progress. The strongly positive impacts of work experience have been communicated to us in private conversations with Kling (2003).

22. FPI employs about 23,000 inmates in federal facilities. About 65,000 inmates (only about 5 percent of all inmates) work in state facilities, and less than 4,000 of these are employed by private-sector companies.

23. H.R. 1577, cosponsored by Representatives Jim Sensenbrenner (R-WI) and Barney Frank (D-MA), would restrict FPI and enhance competition for FPI products from private suppliers. Private-sector employment is also limited by other restrictions in the Prison Industries Enhancement legislation of 1979, such as requirements that inmates be paid "prevailing wages" in local areas.

24. Freeman (1996) has estimated that the costs of crime and incarceration in the U.S.—based on the direct costs of administering prisons and the criminal justice systems as well as the indirect costs of forgone earnings—might be as high as 4 percent of gross domestic product, or over $400 billion annually.

7

Summary and Conclusion

Nearly three million less-educated young people between the ages of 16 and 24—about half of whom are young men—are disconnected from education and employment in the United States. For some groups, like young black men, the low rates of employment and high rates of illegal activity and incarceration are particularly disturbing. While welfare reform and related efforts have addressed some of the issues related to disconnected young women, young men have received less attention in policy circles. Accordingly, employment rates among young low-income women improved during the 1990s while those among young men continued to worsen. The effects of low incomes and high crime and incarceration rates are borne not only by the young men themselves, but also by their families and children, their communities, and the nation as a whole—which pays an enormous price to administer a massive prison system, and is also denied the productive labor of so many of its young men.

What set of policies—federal, state, and local—would help to reconnect these young men to successful lives and prevent further disconnection in the future? To answer this question, we began our study by considering the characteristics of disconnected young men—by race and ethnicity, by educational attainment, and over time. We also reviewed ongoing trends and likely prospects in the nation's labor market. Furthermore, we considered other pieces of the policy context, such as the fiscal constraints America faces in the years to come as baby boomers begin retiring and current surpluses in retirement programs are drawn down.

Our review of these factors led us to focus on three broad areas of youth policy: (1) expanding education and training; (2) improving the financial incentives to work for younger, less-skilled individuals; and (3) addressing specific barriers facing particular groups of youth, such as noncustodial fathers and ex-offenders.

This chapter summarizes the evidence and discusses what we do and do not know from experience with and evaluations of programmatic efforts to date. In addition, we recapitulate our policy recommendations. Finally, we say a few words about how to get started on our policy agenda, and what policymakers at all levels can do.

Again, our focus is far from comprehensive. We have not examined in depth the solutions to those aspects of disconnection affected by discrimination. We have plumbed neither the full range of policies nor the panoply of civic and private actions that would prevent and remedy disconnection. Furthermore, we have not examined exhaustively the measures that would help families function more effectively, reduce negative cultural influences, and support individuals in assuming personal responsibility for their behavior. Nonetheless, our suggestions can make an important difference toward reducing the incidence of disconnection.

Characteristics of Disconnected Young Men and the Labor Market

The number of disconnected young men reflects underlying school enrollment and employment patterns and trends among young people in the nation. Both enrollment and employment rates have grown in recent years among less-educated women but have grown less or declined among their male counterparts. In fact, school enrollment rates of young women exceed those of young men in each racial and ethnic group that we examined. Employment of young low-income women in the past decade has increased, influenced by policy initiatives such as welfare reform and the growth of income supports for working custodial parents (e.g., subsidized child care and the earned income tax credit [EITC]). While idleness among young women is often related to marriage or childrearing, the same seems not to be true among young men.

Of all groups, young African-American men have the lowest employment rates and the highest rates of disconnection—particularly when we include incarcerated young men. Indeed, young black men are the only group for whom employment declined and disconnection rose throughout the 1990s—a situation at least partly caused by their very high incarceration rates and by the stricter enforcement of child support policies, which seems to drive low-income men out of the labor market. While young Hispanic men, especially immigrants, work at high rates, their school attendance and completion rates lag seriously behind those of young whites and blacks.

Educational attainment and test scores for minorities, especially African Americans, fall below those for nonminorities and, in a labor market where demand has clearly shifted away from less-skilled workers, these "achievement gaps" contribute to African Americans' lower employment and earnings relative to whites. But, at any level of education or test scores, the employment rates of young African-American men (and, to a lesser extent, Hispanic men) lag well behind those of whites for a variety of reasons, including discrimination, "spatial mismatch," weak employment networks, and negative peer culture.

In the labor market, employment and wages have risen most rapidly in jobs where higher education and cognitive skill needs are greatest. At the same time, considerable future hiring will likely occur in various occupational and industrial categories (particularly in health care, construction, transportation, wholesale trade, and some parts of manufacturing) where educational needs are more modest, and—at least in some cases—where wages are at or near the national average. As baby boomer retirements begin to unfold, a great deal of "replacement hiring" will take place in those sectors, even if little net new growth is occurring. Economic studies also continue to show strong labor market returns for early work experience and on-the-job training, even for those without college degrees.

We therefore conclude that, while improving achievement and postsecondary educational attainment among minorities and low-income groups is vitally important, we also need to improve occupational skills, early work experience, and labor market contacts among those in high school for whom college education seems unlikely. At the same time, we recognize that wages will remain meager for some members of these groups, increasing the likelihood that they will disconnect from school and work at an early age. Furthermore, some groups, like ex-offenders and young noncustodial fathers, will face particular problems becoming or remaining employed, and may benefit from enhanced incentives to seek or accept such employment.

Accordingly, we have focused on a range of *education and training* approaches for adolescents, teens, and young adults—with particular attention paid to the high school years. We also have advocated *improving the incentives to work* among those facing low wages, by raising the minimum wage and providing subsidies or tax credits to young men with low earnings, and *reducing barriers* associated with previous incarceration and noncustodial parenthood.

Education and Training

We reviewed four components of education and training policy, which vary with the ages and personal circumstances of the youth served. These four components include (1) youth development initiatives, such as after-school and mentoring programs for teens; (2) high school reforms and improvements, including career and technical education (CTE), school-to-career approaches (such as apprenticeships), and independent charter and alternative schools for at-risk youth or those who have already dropped out; (3) community colleges, and especially their efforts to reach out to low-income youth; and (4) training programs for disadvantaged out-of-school youth. We also described other training programs that focus by career sector on matching employers and potential workers, and could be applied more widely to younger people.

Within most of these areas we identified approaches and programs that have been rigorously evaluated and are cost-effective. These include youth development programs, such as Big Brothers Big Sisters (and, to some extent, Quantum Opportunities); school-to-work programs, such as the Career Academies; postschool training programs, such as the Job Corps and Youth Service Corps; and programs for adults, such as the Center for Employment and Training in San Jose. Other initiatives—such as the Harlem Children's Zone or YouthBuild—have not yet been rigorously evaluated but appear quite promising on the basis of demonstrated outcomes. Many other approaches—particularly in areas such as alternative education—are intriguing to us, but currently offer little evidence on outcomes or impacts.

We also mentioned other policies that seem compelling in light of labor market trends and other bodies of evidence. A strong case exists for greater funding of Pell Grants, and for loosening restrictions that deny such grants to people with criminal convictions. Furthermore, more federal support could be provided for employer-sponsored apprenticeships and internships that would further bridge the gaps between school and the workplace.

Finally, we considered the need to develop not only particular education and training programs, but also to build effective community-wide systems for youth. The Harlem Children's Zone is one example of a private, local effort that provides comprehensive services at an impressive scale. The After School Matters (ASM) program in Chicago exemplifies a similar, city-sponsored effort. The U.S. Department of Labor's Youth Opportunities (YO) program is a federal initiative to fund such efforts in 36 low-income communities across the country.

On the basis of our review, we propose the following:

- Funding should increase for proven programs, such as the Job Corps, Youth Service Corps, Career Academies, and similar efforts. Federal funding for youth programs should be gradually and continually increased, both in programs with dedicated funding (e.g., the Job Corps and YouthBuild) and also in formula and competitive streams under the Workforce Investment Act. Funding for CTE and school-to-career efforts should be maintained under the Perkins Act, though perhaps with less formula funding and more distribution through competitive grants. At the same time, states and localities should be encouraged (through technical assistance, revised performance standards, etc.) to allocate formula funding in new ways that make greater use of effective models. In addition, Pell Grant funding should increase and be made available to ex-offenders.

- The federal government should continue to encourage the development of local community-wide education and training systems, building on the achievements and lessons generated by the Youth Opportunity programs. Existing YO sites should continue to be funded and upgraded, and new sites should be added. A focus on building local infrastructure and on improving incentives for local governments to track disconnected young people is especially important.

- The Labor Department should develop a new program to support employer-provided apprenticeships and internships, with significant direct employer involvement in the development of standards for education and training and their implementation.

- An aggressive program of rigorous evaluation should be undertaken by the U.S. Departments of Labor and Education, especially with regard to charter schools and alternative schooling models such as blending high school and community college attendance for those with poor academic records.

Improving Financial Incentives

The research evidence suggests clearly that labor force activity among less-educated young men has decreased since the 1970s, partly because of declining wages. At the same time, large increases in the EITC for low-income custodial parents in the 1980s and early 1990s improved the labor force participation rates among single mothers. Other programs such as New Hope, which guaranteed employment and benefits (such as health care) to low-income workers, also generated some increases in labor market activity among young men.

Accordingly, we recommend a major effort to raise the earnings of low-income men. Raising federal and state minimum wages is one way of accomplishing this goal. While this approach may discourage some employers from hiring less-skilled youth, we believe that taking care not to make such increases precipitous will keep such risks to a minimum while encouraging young men to become and remain attached to the labor market. Thus, we propose the following:

- The federal minimum wage should be increased to roughly 45 percent of the mean average wage in the economy for production workers (which currently would be roughly $7 per hour), and should not be allowed to fall significantly below that level in the future.
- States should raise their own minimum wages if the federal government does not, especially as labor markets tighten.

Another way to raise the earnings of less-skilled workers is through publicly financed subsidies or tax credits. These measures might not focus on youth per se but would encourage youth to remain connected to school and work as they look to and prepare for adulthood. Options for doing so include

- a broad-based subsidy for low-wage workers, which pays some fraction (perhaps half) of the difference between a target wage and all wages below that level;

- a major increase in the EITC for childless adults; or
- an extension of the EITC targeted to low-income noncustodial parents who are paying all or most of their current child support payments.

The broad-based wage subsidy would be by far the most expensive of these approaches, and would provide benefits to many low-wage workers who are not necessarily in low-income families. Basing the EITC on family income eliminates this problem, but generates a "marriage tax" by discouraging the formation of two-parent families in which both parents work, and where low-income single parents are more likely to lose eligibility for the credit if they get married. This problem can, however, be ameliorated in various ways, such as by treating second earners differently from first earners in computing total family income.

Targeting the EITC to noncustodial fathers is the least expensive approach, and administratively feasible. Some might think that it rewards those who have fathered unwed children, but we believe that, on balance, it would encourage more employment among noncustodial parents, more support for their children, better parenting among noncustodial fathers, and less crime. Thus, while we prefer the broader extension of the EITC, we argue at least for its more modest extension to noncustodial fathers in the short term.

Reducing Barriers Facing Noncustodial Fathers and Ex-Offenders

In the African-American community in particular, young men are quite likely to be noncustodial fathers and to have prison records. Indeed, by age 34, up to one-half of black men are noncustodial fathers and perhaps 30 percent have been to prison. We uncovered strong evidence that both of these factors discourage labor force participation. Prevention strategies are needed to reduce the incidence of births outside of marriage and of incarceration rates; our suggestions mostly address the current realities of high incarceration and unwed fatherhood.

Noncustodial fathers face fairly steep child support orders relative to their income. Their obligations are often set in absentia and by judges with no knowledge of these fathers' personal earnings capacities. Arrears pile up frequently, especially among those who are incarcerated, and up to 65 percent of earnings can be garnished to pay these arrears. Furthermore, much of child support payments are not "passed through" to families by the states, further lessening incentives for low-income men to work in the formal economy and meet these obligations.

Young offenders face a range of impediments to school and work. In many ways these obstacles parallel those faced by adults with criminal records—poor skills, mental health and substance abuse problems, and employers' reluctance to hire them. However, young men (and occasionally women) with criminal records deal with additional complications, such as dependence on their families and uncertainty whether they will be accepted back in school. The fragmentation and disconnection among the criminal justice system, schools, employers, and local government compound these difficulties and allow many young offenders to fall through the cracks with minimal support or supervision.

To deal with issues facing noncustodial parents, we suggest

- reconsidering the processes by which child support orders are established for low-income fathers, and also the levels at which they are set;
- promoting arrearage forgiveness options for low-income fathers who are making good-faith efforts to meet their current orders;
- encouraging more states to pass through income collected from noncustodial parents to their low-income families; and
- piloting and evaluating efforts to provide greater employment assistance to low-income fathers—including public employment options and stipends for periods when fathers are in training.

Whether the federal government or the states should take the lead on these items is less clear to us, but guidance and support from the federal government would surely be helpful in stimulating state-level policy changes.

For young offenders, we recommend

- expanding opportunities for education, training, and work experience for young offenders while they are still incarcerated;
- providing more funding for prisoner reentry efforts, with particular set-asides for young offenders;
- setting an aggressive evaluation agenda of school, employment, and aftercare programs for young offenders (taking care, as in any area, not to draw policy conclusions prematurely from data not gathered over a long enough time period); and

- developing institutional links between the criminal justice system and other institutions, such as schools, employers, and community organizations, along with establishing clearer incentives for these groups to monitor the progress of young offenders after release.

Getting from Here to There—or At Least Getting Started

Our proposed policy agenda is fairly ambitious. We have no illusions that this list of recommendations will be completely enacted any time soon. We understand the fiscal constraints under which the federal government now operates—and that these constraints will likely become more serious during the next several years. We also understand the political forces that might limit the complete endorsement of such an agenda at any level of government, even under better fiscal circumstances.

However, it would be a tragic error for the federal government not to invest new resources in our youth. We do not disagree with the call in the 2003 White House Task Force report for better coordination among and management of existing youth programs; however, even under the best management circumstances, the resources currently being expended fall far short of the needs. Critical to the progress on employment among young single mothers that occurred in the 1990s was the investment of tens of billions of dollars into employment supports for these women—expansions of the EITC, child care expenditures, and the reallocation of funds from cash assistance to work supports under the Temporary Assistance for Needy Families program. The increases we envision for low-income youth would be much smaller than those initiatives, and would be trivial in comparison with the overall federal budget. Yet, they could still make important differences for disconnected youth.

At the same time, we recognize that the amount of additional federal spending forthcoming over the next several years might be limited. Therefore, concerned state and local policymakers should take their own steps to address these problems. We have outlined a set of policies—on education and training options (and especially the building of youth systems), on child support programs, and on programmatic efforts for young offenders—where state and local leaders can begin to implement new strategies even in the absence of federal leadership.

Some of these activities—particularly in education and training—involve using existing funding streams to embrace cost-effective programs and to build systems at the community level. Others—such as the review of state-level laws and policies regarding child support and offenders in the labor market—will require political will rather than significant new financial resources. Important constituencies must be mobilized for all of this to occur, and an appropriate balance between policy activism and caution will need to be struck as we await new evaluation results.

We also hope that, as labor markets recover from the downturn of the early 2000s, and as baby boomers begin to retire, the short supplies of skilled labor (relative to demand) will become more apparent to policymakers, civic leaders, and employers. Perhaps this situation will motivate previously unwilling groups to push for and undertake a set of new initiatives for and investments in youth.

The problems for low-income and disconnected youth have always been serious, but the costs that these entail for the rest of the country will likely grow. Perhaps this realization, more than any other, will motivate us to confront the issue of disconnected youth head-on, with more seriousness and more vigor than ever before.

References

After School Matters. 2004. http://www.afterschoolmatters.org.

Altschuler, David, and Rachel Brash. 2003. "Adolescent and Teenage Offenders Confronting the Challenges and Opportunities of Reentry." Paper presented at the Roundtable on Youth Reentry, The Urban Institute, Washington, DC, May 28–29.

American Youth Policy Forum and the Center for Workforce Development, Institute for Educational Leadership. 2000. "Looking Forward: School-to-Work Principles and Strategies for Sustainability." American Youth Policy Forum Report. Washington, DC: American Youth Policy Forum.

Annie E. Casey Foundation. 2004. *Kids Count 2004 Data Book.* Baltimore, MD: Annie E. Casey Foundation.

Applebaum, Eileen, Annette Bernhardt, and Richard J. Murnane, eds. 2003. *Low-Wage America: How Employers Are Reshaping Opportunity in the Workplace.* New York: Russell Sage Foundation.

Aron, Laudan, and Janine Zweig. 2003. "Towards a Typology of Alternative Education Programs: A Compilation of Elements from the Literature." Prepared for the Roundtable on Alternative Education for Disconnected Youth, The Urban Institute, Washington, DC, May 13.

Aspen Institute. 2002. "Growing Together or Growing Apart." Aspen Institute Domestic Strategies Group Report. Washington, DC: The Aspen Institute.

———. 2004. "Discussion Paper for Meeting on Sectoral Initiatives." Prepared for the Meeting on Sectoral Initiatives, Washington, DC, April 21–23.

Association of Career and Technical Educators. 2004. "Frequently Asked Questions." http://www.acteonline.org/career_tech/faq.cfm.

Atkinson, Robert, and Knut Rostad. 2003. "Can Inmates Become an Integral Part of the U.S. Workforce?" Paper presented at the Urban Institute Youth Reentry Roundtable, Washington, DC, May 19–20.

Autor, David H., and Mark G. Duggan. 2003. "The Rise in the Disability Rolls and the Decline in Unemployment." *Quarterly Journal of Economics* 118(1): 157–205.

Bailey, Thomas, and Melinda Mechur Karp. 2003. "Promoting College Access and Success: A Review of Credit-Based Transition Programs." Community College Research Center Report. New York: Teachers College, Columbia University.

Bassi, Laurie, and Jens Ludwig. 2000. "School-to-Work Programs in the United States: A Multi-Firm Case Study of Training, Benefits, and Costs." *Industrial and Labor Relations Review* 53(2): 219–39.

Becker, Gary. 1975. *Human Capital,* 2nd ed. Chicago: University of Chicago Press.

Bernstein, Jared, and John Schmitt. 1998. "Making Work Pay: The Impact of the 1996–97 Minimum Wage Increase." Economic Policy Institute Report. Washington, DC: Economic Policy Institute.

Berrien, Jenny, and Christopher Winship. 2003. "Should We Have Faith in the Churches? Ten Point Coalition's Effect on Boston's Youth Violence." In *Guns, Crime, and Punishment in America,* edited by Bernard E. Harcourt (222–48). New York: New York University Press.

Besharov, Douglas J., ed. 1999. *America's Disconnected Youth: Toward a Preventive Strategy.* Washington, DC: CWLA Press.

Betanzos, Amelia. 2003. "Youth Violence, Schools, and Management: A Personal Reflection across the Sectors." In *Securing Our Children's Future,* edited by Gary S. Katzmann (287–304). Washington, DC: Brookings Institution Press.

Bishop, John. 1996. "Is the College Graduate Labor Market Headed for a Bust? A Critique of Job Requirements Projections." *New England Economic Review* May/June: 115–35.

Bishop, John, and Ferran Mane. 2004. "The Impacts of Career-Technical Education on High School Completion and Labor Market Success." Cornell University, Ithaca, NY. Unpublished.

Blank, Rebecca, and Jonah Gelbach. 2002. "Are Less-Skilled Women Crowding Out Labor Force Participation among Less-Skilled Men?" Paper presented at the Extending Opportunities Conference, Washington, DC, May 24.

Blank, Rebecca, and Ron Haskins, eds. 2001. *The New World of Welfare.* Washington, DC: Brookings Institution Press.

Blank, Rebecca, and Lucie Schmidt. 2001. "Work, Wages, and Welfare." In *The New World of Welfare,* edited by Rebecca Blank and Ron Haskins (70–102). Washington, DC: Brookings Institution Press.

Blau, Francine, and Lawrence Kahn. 1997. "Swimming Upstream: Trends in the Gender Wage Differential in the 1980s." *Journal of Labor Economics* 15(1): 1, 1–42.

Blau, Francine, Lawrence Kahn, and Jane Waldfogel. 2000. "Understanding Young Women's Marriage Decisions." *Industrial and Labor Relations Review* 53(4): 624–47.

Bloom, Howard, James Riccio, and Nandita Verma. 2005. "Promoting Work in Public Housing: The Effectiveness of Jobs-Plus." MDRC Report. New York: MDRC.

Borjas, George J. 1996. *Labor Economics.* New York: McGraw Hill.

Bos, Johannes, Thomas Brock, Greg Duncan, Robert Granger, Aletha Huston, and Vonnie McLoyd. 1999. "New Hope for People with Low Incomes: Two Year Results of a Program to Reduce Poverty and Reform Welfare." MRDC Report. New York: MDRC.

Bottoms, Gene. 2003. "Choices Within a Strong Academic Framework." In *Shaping the Future of American Youth: Youth Policy in the 21st Century,* edited by Anne Lewis (8–10). Washington, DC: American Youth Policy Forum.

Bound, John. 1986. "Appendix: NBER-Mathematica Survey of Inner-City Black Youth: An Analysis of the Undercount of Older Youths." In *The Black Youth Employment Crisis,* edited by Richard B. Freeman and Harry J. Holzer (443–57). Chicago: University of Chicago Press.

Bound, John, and Harry J. Holzer. 1993. "Industrial Shifts, Skill Levels and the Labor Market for White and Black Males." *Review of Economics and Statistics* 75(3): 387–94.

Braga, Anthony A., and David M. Kennedy. 2002. "Reducing Gang Violence in Boston." In *Responding to Gangs: Evaluation and Research,* edited by Winifred L. Reed and Scott H. Decker (264–88). Washington, DC: National Institute of Justice.

Brand, Betsy. 2003. "Rigor and Relevance: A New Vision for Career and Technical Education." American Youth Policy Forum White Paper. Washington, DC: American Youth Policy Forum.

Brown, Charles. 1999. "Minimum Wages, Employment, and Distribution of Income." In *Handbook of Labor Economics,* vol. 3B, edited by Orley C. Ashenfelter and David Card (2102–58). Amsterdam: North-Holland.

Buck, Maria L. 2000. "Getting Back to Work: Employment Programs for Ex-Offenders." Public/Private Ventures Field Report. Philadelphia: Public/Private Ventures.

Bushway, Shawn. 2003. "Reentry and Prison Work Programs." Paper presented at the Urban Institute Youth Reentry Roundtable, Washington, DC, May 19–20.

Bushway, Shawn, Shauna Briggs, Meridith Thanner, Faye Taxman, and Mischelle Van Brakle. 2004. "Private Providers of Criminal History Records: Do You Get What You Pay For?" Paper presented at the Russell Sage Foundation Working Group Session on Employment and Reentry, New York, May 19–20.

Cameron, Stephen, and James Heckman. 1993. "The Nonequivalence of High School Equivalents." *Journal of Labor Economics* 11(1): 1–47.

Cannon, Angie. 2004. "Juvenile Injustice." *US News and World Report,* August 9.

Card, David, and Dean R. Hyslop. 2005. "Estimating the Effects of a Time-Limited Earnings Subsidy for Welfare Leavers: The Self-Sufficiency Project." Social Research and Demonstration Corporation Working Paper Series 05-02. http://www.srdc.org/english/publications/card_hyslop.pdf.

Card, David, and Alan G. Krueger. 1995. *Myth and Measurement: The New Economics of the Minimum Wage.* Princeton, NJ: Princeton University Press.

Carnevale, Anthony, and Donna Desrochers. 2001. *Help Wanted . . . Credentials Required: Community Colleges in the Knowledge Economy.* Washington, DC: Educational Testing Service.

Chasanov, Amy. 2004. "No Longer Getting By: An Increase in the Minimum Wage Is Long Overdue." Economic Policy Institute Research and Ideas Working Paper. Washington, DC: Economic Policy Institute.

Choitz, Victoria, and Rebecca Widom. 2003. *Money Matters: How Financial Aid Affects Nontraditional Students in Community Colleges.* New York: MDRC.

Cohen, Marie, and Douglas J. Besharov. 2004. *The Important Role of Career and Technical Education: Implications for Federal Policy.* Unpublished.

Connell, James P., Anne C. Kubisch, Lisbeth B. Schorr, and Carol H. Weiss, eds. 1995. *New Approaches to Evaluating Community Initiatives.* Washington, DC: The Aspen Institute.

Cook, Philip J., and Jens Ludwig. 1998. "The Burdens of 'Acting White': Do Black Adolescents Disparage Academic Achievement?" In *The Black-White Test Score Gap,* edited by Christopher Jencks and Meredith Phillips (375–400). Washington, DC: Brookings Institution Press.

Crigger, Joan. 2004. "Workforce Directors Meet in Kansas City (MO) to Share Ideas on What's Next for Youth Opportunity Communities." *U.S. Mayor,* January 12. http://www.usmayors.org/uscm/us_mayor_newspaper/documents/01_12_04/workforce.asp.

Cullen, Francis T., and Paul Gendreau. 2000. "Assessing Correctional Rehabilitation: Policy, Practice, and Prospects." In *Criminal Justice 2000: Policies, Processes, and Decisions of the Criminal Justice System,* vol. 3, edited by Julie Horney (109–75). Washington, DC: National Institute of Justice.

Department of Youth and Community Development. 2004. "Out-of-School Time Programs: The Beacon Program." http://www.ci.nyc.ny.us/html/dycd/html/services-afterschool-beacon.html.

Dickens, William T. 2005. "Genetic Differences and School Readiness." *The Future of Children* 15(1): 55–69.

Eberwein, Curt, John Ham, and Robert LaLonde. 1997. "The Impact of Classroom Training on the Employment Histories of Disadvantaged Women: Evidence from Experimental Data." *Review of Economic Studies* 64(4): 655–82.

Eccles, Jacquelynne, and Jennifer Appleton Gootman, eds. 2002. *Community Programs to Promote Youth Development.* Washington, DC: National Academy Press.

Ellen, Ingrid Gould, and Margery Austin Turner. 1997. "Does Neighborhood Matter? Assessing Recent Evidence." *Housing Policy Debate* 8(4): 833–66.

Ellwood, David T. 1982. "Teenage Unemployment: Permanent Scars or Temporary Blemishes?" In *The Youth Labor Market Problem: Its Nature, Causes, and Consequences,* edited by Richard B. Freeman and David A. Wise (349–90). Chicago: University of Chicago Press.

———. 2001. "The Impact of the Earned Income Tax Credit and Social Policy Reform on Work, Marriage, and Living Arrangements." *National Tax Journal* 53(4): 2, 1063–1106.

Ellwood, David T., and Christopher Jencks. 2004. "The Uneven Spread of Single-Parent Families: What Do We Know? Where Do We Look for Answers?" In *Social Inequality,* edited by Kathryn M. Neckerman (3–78). New York: Russell Sage Foundation.

Falcón, Luis M., and Edwin Melendez. 2001. "Racial and Ethnic Differences in Job Searching in Urban Centers." In *Urban Inequality: Evidence from Four Cities,* edited by Alice O'Connor, Chris Tilly, and Lawrence D. Bobo (341–71). New York: Russell Sage Foundation.

Ferguson, Ronald F. 2001. "Test Score Trends Along Racial Lines, 1971 to 1996: Popular Culture and Community Academic Standards." In *America Becoming: Racial Trends and their Consequences,* vol. 1, edited by Neil J. Smelser, William Julius Wilson, and Faith Mitchell (348–90). Washington, DC: National Academy Press.

Filer, Randall K., Daniel S. Hamermesh, and Albert E. Rees. 1996. *The Economics of Work and Pay,* 6th ed. New York: Harper Collins.

Fix, Michael E., and Raymond J. Struyk. 1993. *Clear and Convincing Evidence: Measurement of Discrimination in America.* Washington, DC: Urban Institute Press.

Freeman, Richard B. 1992. "Crime and the Employment of Disadvantaged Youth." In *Urban Labor Markets and Job Opportunity,* edited by George E. Peterson and Wayne Vroman (201–38). Washington, DC: Urban Institute Press.

———. 1996. "Why Do So Many Young American Men Commit Crimes and What Might We Do About It?" *Journal of Economic Perspectives* 10(1): 25–42.

———. 2003. "Ex-Offenders: Closing the Revolving Door." Paper presented at New York University Reentry Roundtable, New York, May 19–20.

Freeman, Richard B., and William M. Rodgers III. 2000. "Area Economic Conditions and the Labor-Market Outcomes of Young Black Men in the 1990s Expansion." In *Prosperity for All? The Economic Boom and African Americans,* edited by Robert Cherry and William M. Rodgers III (50–87). New York: Russell Sage Foundation.

Furstenberg, Frank F., Thomas D. Cook, Robert Sampson, and Gail Slap. 2002. "Early Adulthood in Cross-National Perspective: Preface." *The Annals of the American Academy of Political and Social Science* 580(1): 6–15.

Giloth, Robert P., ed. 2003. *Workforce Intermediaries for the Twenty-first Century.* Philadelphia: Temple University Press.

Grogger, Jeffrey. 1998. "Market Wages and Youth Crime." *Journal of Labor Economics* 16(4): 756–91.

Grubb, Norton W. 1996. *Learning to Work: The Case for Reintegrating Job Training and Education.* New York: Russell Sage Foundation.

Hahn, Andrew. 1999. "Extending the Time of Learning." In *America's Disconnected Youth: Toward a Preventive Strategy,* edited by Douglas J. Besharov (233–66). Washington, DC: CWLA Press.

———. 2003. "Making Sure There Are No Cracks." In *Shaping the Future of American Youth: Youth Policy in the 21st Century,* edited by Anne Lewis (54–57). Washington, DC: American Youth Policy Forum.

Hamilton, Stephen, Mary Agnes Hamilton, and Karen Pittman. 2004. "Principles for Youth Development." In *The Youth Development Handbook: Coming of Age in American Communities,* edited by Stephen Hamilton and Mary Agnes Hamilton (3–22). Thousand Oaks, CA: SAGE Publications.

Harhoff, Dietmar, and Thomas J. Kane. 1997. "Is the German Apprenticeship System a Panacea for the U.S. Labor Market?" *Journal of Population Economics* 10(2): 171–96.

Harlem Children's Zone. 2004. http://www.hcz.org.

Hecker, Daniel. 2004. "Occupational Employment Projections to 2012." *Monthly Labor Review* 127(2): 80–105.

Heckman, James, Robert LaLonde, and Jeffrey Smith. 1999. "The Economics and Econometrics of Active Labor Market Programs." In *Handbook of Labor Economics,* vol. 3A, edited by Orley C. Ashenfelter and David Card (1865–2097). Amsterdam: North-Holland.

Heclo, Hugh. 2002. "The Politics of Welfare Reform." In *The New World of Welfare,* edited by Rebecca Blank and Ron Haskins (169–200). Washington, DC: Brookings Institution Press.

Holzer, Harry J. 1986. "Reservation Wages and Their Labor Market Effects for Black and White Male Youth." *Journal of Human Resources* 21(2): 157–77.

———. 1987. "Informal Job Search and Black Youth Unemployment." *American Economic Review* 77(3): 446–52.

———. 1996. *What Employers Want: Job Prospects for Less-Educated Workers.* New York: Russell Sage Foundation.

Holzer, Harry J., and Robert LaLonde. 2000. "Job Change and Job Stability among Less-Skilled Young Workers." In *Finding Jobs: Work and Welfare Reform,* edited by David Card and Rebecca Blank (125–59). New York: Russell Sage Foundation.

Holzer, Harry J., and Paul Offner. 2002. "Trends in Employment Outcomes of Young Black Men, 1979–2000." Institute for Research on Poverty Discussion Paper 1247-02. Madison, WI: Institute for Research on Poverty, University of Wisconsin–Madison.

Holzer, Harry J., Paul Offner, and Elaine Sorensen. 2005. "Declining Employment among Young Black Less-Educated Men: The Role of Incarceration and Child Support." *Journal of Policy Analysis and Management* 24(2): 329–50.

Holzer, Harry J., Steven Raphael, and Michael Stoll. 2004. "Will Employers Hire Ex-Offenders? Employer Preferences, Background Checks, and Their Determinants." In *The Impact of Incarceration on Families and Communities,* edited by Mary Patillo, David Weiman, and Bruce Western (205–46). New York: Russell Sage Foundation.

Holzer, Harry J., Richard Block, Marcus Cheatham, and Jack H. Knott. 1993. "Are Training Subsidies for Firms Effective? The Michigan Experience." *Industrial and Labor Relations Review* 46(4): 677–90.

Hotz, V. Joseph, Guido N. Imbens, and Jacob A. Klerman. 2000. "The Long-Term Gains from GAIN: A Re-Analysis of the Impacts of the California GAIN Program." National Bureau of Economic Research Working Paper No. 8007. Cambridge, MA: National Bureau of Economic Research.

Hughes, Katherine L., Thomas R. Bailey, and Melinda J. Mechur. 2001. "School-to-Work: Making a Difference in Education." Institute on Education and the Economy Research Report. New York: Institute on Education and the Economy, Columbia University.

Huston, Aletha C., Cynthia Miller, Lashawn Richburg-Hayes, Greg J. Duncan, Carolyn A. Eldred, Thomas S. Weisner, Edward Lowe, Vonnie C. McLoyd, Danielle A. Crosby, Marika N. Ripke, and Cindy Redcross. 2003. "New Hope for Families and Children: Five-Year Results of a Program to Reduce Poverty and Reform Welfare." MDRC Research Report. http://www.mdrc.org/publications/345/full.pdf.

Ihlanfeldt, Keith R., and David L. Sjoquist. 1998. "The Spatial Mismatch Hypothesis: A Review of Recent Studies and Their Implications for Welfare Reform." *Housing Policy Debate* 9(4): 849–92.

Ivry, Robert, and Fred Doolittle. 2003. "Improving the Economic and Life Outcomes of At-Risk Youth." MDRC Concept Paper. New York: MDRC.

James, Donna Walker, ed. 1997. *Some Things Do Make a Difference for Youth: A Compendium of Evaluations of Youth Programs and Practices.* Washington, DC: American Youth Policy Forum.

Jargowsky, Paul A. 1997. *Poverty and Place: Ghettos, Barrios, and the American City.* New York: Russell Sage Foundation.

———. 2003. "Stunning Progress, Hidden Problems: The Dramatic Decline of Concentrated Poverty in the 1990s." Washington, DC: The Brookings Institution. *Living Cities Census Series* Policy Brief.

Jastrzab, JoAnn, John Blomquist, Julie Masker, and Larry Orr. 1997. "Youth Corps: Promising Strategies for Young People and their Communities." Studies in Workforce Development and Income Security Report No. 1-97. Cambridge, MA: Abt Associates Inc.

Jencks, Christopher, and Meredith Phillips, eds. 1998. *The Black-White Test Score Gap*. Washington, DC: Brookings Institution Press.

Johnson, William R., and Derek Neal. 1998. "Basic Skills and the Black-White Earnings Gap." In *The Black-White Test Score Gap*, edited by Christopher Jencks and Meredith Phillips (480–98). Washington, DC: Brookings Institution Press.

Juhn, Chinhui. 1992. "Decline of Male Labor Market Participation: The Role of Declining Market Opportunities." *Quarterly Journal of Economics* 107(1): 79–122.

Juhn, Chinhui, Kevin Murphy, and Robert Topel. 1991. "Why Has the Natural Rate of Unemployment Increased through Time?" *Brookings Papers on Economic Activity* 2: 75–142.

Juvenile Reintegration and Aftercare Center. 2004. "Juvenile Reintegration and Aftercare Center, Intensive Juvenile Aftercare Reference Guide." http://www.csus.edu/ssis/cdcps/IntensiveAftercareReferenceGuide.pdf.

Katz, Lawrence F. 1998. "Wage Subsidies for the Disadvantaged." In *Generating Jobs: How to Increase Demand for Less-Skilled Workers*, edited by Peter Gottschalk and Richard Freeman (21–53). New York: Russell Sage Foundation.

Katz, Lawrence F., and David H. Autor. 1999. "Changes in the Wage Structure and Earnings Inequality." In *Handbook of Labor Economics*, vol. 3A, edited by Orley C. Ashenfelter and David Card (1463–1555). Amsterdam: North-Holland.

Katz, Lawrence F., Jeffrey Kling, and Jeffrey B. Liebman. 2001. "Moving to Opportunity in Boston: Early Results of a Randomized Mobility Experiment." *Quarterly Journal of Economics* 116(2): 607–54.

Katzmann, Gary S., ed. 2002. *Securing Our Children's Future: New Approaches to Juvenile Justice and Youth Violence*. Washington, DC: Brookings Institution Press.

Kazis, Richard, and Marty Leibowitz. 2003. "Changing Courses: Instructional Innovations That Help Low-Income Students Succeed in Community College." Opening Doors Project Report. New York: MDRC.

Kemple, James. 2004. *Career Academies: Impacts on Labor Market Outcomes and Educational Attainment*. New York: MDRC.

Kemple, James J., and Corinne M. Herlihy. 2004. *The Talent Development High School Model: Context, Components, and Initial Impacts on Ninth-Grade Students' Engagement and Performance*. New York: MDRC.

Kennedy, David. 2002. "A Tale of One City: Reflections on the Boston Gun Project." In *Securing Our Children's Future: New Approaches to Juvenile Justice and Youth Violence*, edited by Gary S. Katzmann (229–61). Washington, DC: Brookings Institution Press.

Kirby, Gretchen, Heather Hill, LaDonna Pavetti, Jon Jacobson, Michelle Derr, and Pamela Winston. 2002. "Transitional Jobs Programs: Stepping Stones to Unsubsidized Employment." Mathematica Research Paper No. PR02-15. Washington, DC: Mathematica Policy Research Inc.

Kirschenman, Joleen, and Kathryn Neckerman. 1991. " 'We'd Love to Hire Them, But . . .' The Meaning of Race for Employers." In *The Urban Underclass*, edited by Christopher Jencks and Paul E. Peterson (203–32). Washington, DC: Brookings Institution Press.

Knox, Virginia, and Cynthia Miller. 2001. "The Challenge of Helping Low-Income Fathers Support Their Children: Final Lessons from Parents' Fair Share." MDRC Research Report. New York: MDRC.

LaLonde, Robert J. 1995. "The Promise of Public Sector–Sponsored Training Programs." *Journal of Economic Perspectives* 9(2): 149–68.

Lattimore, Pamela K., Ann D. Witte, and Joanna R. Baker. 1990. "Experimental Assessment of the Effect of Vocational Training on Youthful Property Offenders." *Evaluation Review* 14: 115–33.

Legler, Paul. 2003. "Low-Income Fathers and Child Support: Starting Off on the Right Track." Policy Studies Inc. Research Report. Denver, CO: Policy Studies Inc.

Lerman, Robert I. 2002. "Helping Out-of-School Youth Attain Labor Market Success: What We Know and How to Learn More." The Urban Institute, Center on Labor, Human Services, and Population, Washington, DC. Unpublished.

———. 2003. "The High-Wage Careers Demonstration Project: A Sectoral Strategy to Improve Outcomes for Workers and Employers." Proposal to the U.S. Department of Labor, The Urban Institute, Center on Labor, Human Services, and Population, Washington, DC.

Levin-Epstein, Jodie, and Mark H. Greenberg, eds. 2003. *Leave No Youth Behind: Opportunities for Congress to Reach Disconnected Youth.* Washington, DC: Center for Law and Social Policy.

Levitt, Steven D. 2004. "Understanding Why Crime Fell in the 1990s: Four Factors that Explain the Decline and Six that Do Not." *Journal of Economic Perspectives* 18(1): 163–90.

Ludwig, Jens, Paul Hirschfeld, and Greg J. Duncan. 2001. "Urban Poverty and Juvenile Crime: Evidence from a Randomized Housing-Mobility Experiment." *Quarterly Journal of Economics* 116(2): 655–79.

Lynch, Lisa M. 1992. "Private-Sector Training and the Earnings of Young Workers." *American Economic Review* 82(1): 299–312.

Mathur, Anita. 2004. "From Jobs to Careers: How California Community College Credentials Pay Off for Welfare Participants." Center for Law and Social Policy Report. Washington, DC: Center for Law and Social Policy.

McConnell, Sheena, and Steven Glazerman. 2001. "National Job Corps Study: The Benefits and Costs of Job Corps." Mathematica Policy Research Report No. PR01-51. Washington, DC: Mathematica Policy Research Inc.

McLanahan, Sara, and Gary Sandefur. 1994. *Growing Up with a Single Parent: What Hurts, What Helps.* Cambridge, MA: Harvard University Press.

Mead, Lawrence M. 2001. "The Politics of Conservative Welfare Reform." In *The New World of Welfare,* edited by Rebecca Blank and Ron Haskins (201–22). Washington, DC: Brookings Institution Press.

Melendez, Edwin. 1996. *Working on Jobs: The Center for Employment Training.* Boston: University of Massachusetts.

Meyer, Daniel R., and Maria Cancian. 2001. "W-2 Child Support Demonstration Evaluation Phase I: Final Report." Institute for Research on Poverty Report. Madison, WI: Institute for Research on Poverty, University of Wisconsin–Madison.

Meyer, Robert H., and David A. Wise. 1982. "High School Preparation and Early Labor Force Experience." In *The Youth Labor Market Problem: Its Nature, Causes, and Consequences,* edited by Richard B. Freeman and David A. Wise (277–348). Chicago: University of Chicago Press.

Michael, Robert T., ed. 2002. *Social Awakening: Adolescent Behavior as Adulthood Approaches.* New York: Russell Sage Foundation.

Michalopoulos, Charles, Doug Tattrie, Cynthia Miller, Philip K. Robins, Pamela Morris, David Gyarmati, Cindy Redcross, Kelly Foley, and Reuben Ford. 2002. *Making Work Pay: Final Report of the Self-Sufficiency Project for Long-Term Welfare Recipients.* Ottawa: Social Research and Demonstration Corporation.

Miller, Cynthia, Johannes M. Bos, Kristin E. Porter, Fannie M. Tseng, Fred C. Doolittle, Deana N. Tanguay, and Mary P. Vencill. 2003. "Working with Disadvantaged Youth: Thirty-Month Findings from the Evaluation of the Center for Employment Training Replication Sites." MDRC Report. New York: MDRC.

Mincy, Ronald. 2002. "Revisiting Jacob's Ladder." Paper presented at Summer Institute on Social Inequality Meetings, John F. Kennedy School of Government, Harvard University, Cambridge, MA, June 15–16.

Moore, Richard W., Daniel R. Blake, G. Michael Phillips, and Daniel McConaughy. 2003. *Training That Works: Lessons from the California Employment and Training Panel Program.* Kalamazoo, MI: W. E. Upjohn Institute for Employment Research.

Moss, Philip, and Chris Tilly. 2001. *Stories Employers Tell: Race, Skill, and Hiring in America.* New York: Russell Sage Foundation.

National Academy Foundation. 2000. *National School-to-Career Conversation: An Agenda for Action.* Washington, DC: National Academy Foundation.

National Campaign to Prevent Teen Pregnancy. 2004. "National Teen Pregnancy and Birth Data." http://www.teenpregnancy.org/resources/data/national.asp.

National Center for Education Statistics. 2002. "Public Alternative Schools and Programs for Students at Risk of Educational Failure: 2000–01." National Center for Education Statistics Statistical Analysis Report. U.S. Department of Education, Washington, DC.

National Governors Association. 2005. "An Action Agenda for Improving America's High Schools." Report released at the National Education Summit on High Schools, Washington, DC, February 26–27. http://www.nga.org/cda/files/0502ACTIONAGENDA.pdf.

Neumark, David, and Rosella Gardecki. 1998. "Order from Chaos? The Effects of Early Labor Market Experiences on Adult Labor Market Outcomes." *Industrial and Labor Relations Review* 51(2): 299–322.

Neumark, David, and William Wascher. 2000. "Comment on 'Minimum Wages and Employment: A Case Study of the Fast-Food Industry in New Jersey and Pennsylvania' by David Card and Alan B. Krueger." *American Economic Review* 90(5): 1362–96.

NewSchools Venture Fund. 2004. "Our Portfolio: High Tech High Learning." http://www.newschools.org/portfolio/hightech.html.

Offner, Paul. 2002. "What's Love Got to Do With It? Why Oprah's Still Single." *The Washington Monthly,* March.

Pager, Devah. 2003. "The Mark of a Criminal Record." *American Journal of Sociology* 108: 937–75.

Pennington, Hilary. 2003. "Building One System for Youth Development and Opportunity." In *Shaping the Future of American Youth: Youth Policy in the 21st Century,* edited by Anne Lewis (59–68). Washington, DC: American Youth Policy Forum.

PEPNet. See Promising and Effective Practices Network.

Pettit, Becky, and Christopher Lyons. 2004. "Status and the Stigma of Incarceration: The Labor Market Effects of Incarceration by Class, Race, and Criminal Involvement."

Paper presented at the Russell Sage Foundation Working Group on Employment and Reentry, New York, May 19–20.

Phelps, Edmund S. 1997. *Rewarding Work: How to Restore Participation and Self-Support to Free Enterprise.* Cambridge, MA: Harvard University Press.

Primus, Wendell. 2002a. "Child Support Policy Changes and Demonstration Projects." Center on Budget and Policy Priorities Report. Washington, DC: Center on Budget and Policy Priorities.

———. 2002b. "Improving Public Policies in Order to Increase the Income and Employment of Low-Income Non-Custodial Fathers." Center on Budget and Policy Priorities Report. Washington, DC: Center on Budget and Policy Priorities.

Promising and Effective Practices Network (PEPNet). 2003. "PEPNet 2003 Profiles: Promising and Effective Practices in Youth Initiatives." PEPNet Report. Washington, DC: National Youth Employment Coalition.

Research and Evaluation Associates. 2002. "DOL Youth Offender Demonstration Project Technical Assistance." http://wdr.doleta.gov/opr/fulltext/yodp_es.pdf.

Rimer, Sarah. 2004. "Last Chance High." *The New York Times,* July 25.

Rivlin, Alice M., and Isabel V. Sawhill. 2004. "How To Balance the Budget." Brookings Institution Policy Brief No. 130. Washington, DC: The Brookings Institution.

Rosenbaum, James E. 1995. "Changing the Geography of Opportunity by Expanding Residential Choice: Lessons from the Gautreaux Program." *Housing Policy Debate* 6(1): 231–69.

———. 2001. *Beyond College for All: Career Paths for the Forgotten Half.* New York: Russell Sage Foundation.

Ruhm, Christopher J. 1997. "Is High School Employment Consumption or Investment?" *Journal of Labor Economics* 15(4): 735–76.

Ryan, Paul. 2001. "The School-to-Work Transition: A Cross-National Perspective." *Journal of Economic Literature* 39(1): 34–92.

Saylor, William, and Gerald Gaes. 1996. *PREP: Training Inmates through Industrial Work Preparation and Vocational and Apprenticeship Instruction.* Washington, DC: U.S. Federal Bureau of Prisons.

Schirm, Allen, Nuria Rodriguez-Planas, Myles Maxfield, and Christina Tuttle. 2003. "The Quantum Opportunities Demonstration: Short-Term Impacts." Mathematica Policy Research Report No. PR03-35. Princeton, NJ: Mathematica Policy Research Inc.

Snyder, Howard. 2003. "An Empirical Portrait of the Youth Reentry Population." Paper presented at the Urban Institute Youth Reentry Roundtable, Washington, DC, May 19–20.

Sorensen, Elaine, and Helen Oliver. 2002. "Policy Reforms Are Needed to Increase Child Support from Poor Fathers." The Urban Institute, Income and Benefits Policy Center, Washington, DC.

Steinberg, Adria, Cheryl Almeida, Lili Allen, and Sue Goldberger. 2003. "Four Building Blocks for a System of Educational Opportunity: Developing Pathways to and through College for Urban Youth." Jobs for the Future Report. Boston: Jobs for the Future.

Steinberg, Laurence, He Len Chung, and Michelle Little. 2003. "Reentry of Adolescents from the Juvenile Justice System: A Developmental Perspective." Paper presented at the Urban Institute Youth Reentry Roundtable, Washington, DC, May 28–29.

Stoneman, Dorothy. 2003. "Flip the Script: Self-Sufficiency and Fulfillment for All." In *Shaping the Future of American Youth: Youth Policy in the 21st Century,* edited by Anne Lewis (41–48). Washington, DC: American Youth Policy Forum.

Sullivan, Eileen, Milton Mino, Katherine Nelson, and Jill Pope. 2002. "Families as a Resource in Recovery from Drug Abuse: An Evaluation of La Bodega de la Familia." Vera Institute of Justice Research Report. New York: Vera Institute of Justice.

Sullivan, Mercer. 2003. "Youth Perspectives on the Experience of Reentry." Paper presented at the Urban Institute Youth Reentry Roundtable, Washington, DC, May 28–29.

Sum, Andrew. 2003. "Left Behind in the Labor Market: Labor Market Problems of the Nation's Out-of-School, Young Adult Population." Northeastern University, Boston. Unpublished.

———. 2004. "Still Young, Restless, and Jobless: The Growing Employment Malaise among U.S. Teens and Young Adults." Northeastern University, Boston. Unpublished.

Swanson, Christopher B. 2004. "Who Graduates? Who Doesn't? A Statistical Portrait of Public High School Graduation." The Urban Institute, Education Policy Center, Washington, DC.

Topel, Robert H., and Michael P. Ward. 1992. "Job Mobility and the Careers of Young Men." *Quarterly Journal of Economics* 107(2): 439–79.

Tough, Paul. 2004. "The Harlem Project." *The New York Times Magazine,* June 20, 44–49.

Travis, Jeremy, and Christy A. Visher. Forthcoming. "Prisoner Reentry and the Pathways to Adulthood: Policy Perspectives." In *On Your Own Without a Net: The Transition to Adulthood for Vulnerable Populations,* edited by D. Wayne Osgood, E. Michael Foster, Constance Flanagan, and Gretchen R. Ruth. Chicago: University of Chicago Press.

Travis, Jeremy, Amy Solomon, and Michelle Waul. 2001. "From Prison to Home: The Dimensions and Consequences of Prisoner Reentry." The Urban Institute, Justice Policy Center, Washington, DC.

Turetsky, Vicki. 2003. "Summary of Child Support, Fatherhood, and Marriage Provisions in House and Senate Versions of H.R. 4." Center for Law and Social Policy Brief. Washington, DC: Center for Law and Social Policy.

Tyler, John H. 2003. "Using State Child Labor Laws to Identify the Effect of School-Year Work on High School Achievement." *Journal of Labor Economics* 21(2): 381–408.

Tyler, John H., and Jeffrey Kling. 2004. "Prison-Based Education and Re-entry into the Mainstream Labor Market." Paper presented at the Russell Sage Foundation Working Group on Employment and Reentry, New York, May 19–20.

Uggen, Christopher. 2000. "Work as a Turning Point in the Life Course of Criminals: A Duration Model of Age, Employment, and Recidivism." *American Sociological Review* 65(4): 529–46.

U.S. Department of Education. 2003. *When Schools Stay Open Late: The National Evaluation of the 21st Century Learning Centers Program, First Year Findings.* Washington, DC: National Center for Education Evaluation and Regional Assistance.

———. 2004. *National Assessment of Vocational Education: Final Report to Congress.* Washington, DC: Office of the Secretary, Policy and Program Studies Service.

———. 2005. http://www.ed.gov.

U.S. Department of Justice, Bureau of Justice Statistics. 2003. "Criminal Offenders Statistics." http://www.ojp.usdoj.gov/bjs/crimoff.htm.

———. 2005. "Additional Corrections Facts at a Glance." http://www.ojp.usdoj.gov/bjs/gcorpop.htm.

U.S. Department of Labor, Bureau of Labor Statistics. 1999. *Futurework: Trends and Challenges for Work in the 21st Century.* Washington, DC: U.S. Government Printing Office.

———. 2004. *Occupational Projections and Training Data: 2004–05 Edition.* Washington, DC: U.S. Government Printing Office.

———. 2005. "Employment Situation." http://www.bls.gov/news.release/empsit.toc.htm.

U.S. General Accounting Office (GAO). 2001. *Registered Apprenticeships: Labor Could Do More to Expand to Other Occupations.* GAO-01-940. Washington, DC: U.S. General Accounting Office.

Wald, Michael, and Tia Martinez. 2003. "Disconnected Youth: An Overview." Hewlett Foundation, Children and Youth Program, Menlo Park, CA. Unpublished.

Walker, Karen, and Amy J. A. Arbreton. 2004. *After-School Pursuits: An Examination of Outcomes in the San Francisco Beacon Initiative.* Philadelphia: Public/Private Ventures.

Waller, Maureen, and Robert Plotnick. 1999. "Child Support and Low-Income Families: Perceptions, Practices, and Policy." Public Policy Institute Report. San Francisco: Public Policy Institute of California.

Warren, Constancia, Michelle Feist, and Nancy Nevarez. 2002. "A Place to Grow: Evaluation of the New York City Beacons." http://scs.aed.org/publications/grow.pdf.

Westat Inc. 2001. *Summary Report: Findings of an Analysis of Household-Based Youth Surveys Conducted in the First Three Youth Opportunity Area Demonstration Sites.* Rockville, MD. Westat.

Western, Bruce, Jeffrey R. Kling, and David F. Weiman. 2001. "The Labor Market Consequences of Incarceration." *Crime and Delinquency* 47(3): 410–427.

White House Task Force for Disadvantaged Youth. 2003. "Final Report." http://www.ncfy.com/disadvantaged/FinalReport.pdf.

Wiebush, Richard G., Betsie McNulty, and Thao Le. 2000. "Implementation of the Intensive Community-Based Aftercare Program." *Juvenile Justice Bulletin,* July. Washington, DC: Office of Juvenile Justice and Delinquency Prevention, U.S. Department of Justice.

Wilson, William Julius. 1987. *The Truly Disadvantaged: The Inner City, The Underclass, and Public Policy.* Chicago: University of Chicago Press.

———. 1996. *When Work Disappears: The World of the New Urban Poor.* New York: Alfred Knopf.

Wisconsin Youth Apprenticeship Program. 2004. "Governor's Work-Based Learning Board: Youth Apprenticeship Program Areas." http://www.dwd.state.wi.us/gwblb/ya_programs.htm.

Young, Jr., Alford A. 2000. "On the Outside Looking In: Low-Income Black Men's Conceptions of Work Opportunities and the 'Good Job.' " In *Coping with Poverty: The Social Contexts of Neighborhood, Work, and Family in the African-American Community,* edited by Sheldon Danziger and Ann Chin Lin (141–71). Ann Arbor: University of Michigan Press.

About the Authors

Peter Edelman is a professor of law and former associate dean for the Georgetown University Law Center. In the Clinton administration, he was assistant secretary for Planning and Evaluation for the Department of Health and Human Services. Among his publications are *Searching for America's Heart: RFK and the Renewal of Hope* (second edition, Georgetown University Press, 2002), the *Atlantic Monthly* article "The Worst Thing Bill Clinton Has Done" (winner of a 1998 Harry Chapin Media Award), and a monthly column in the *Legal Times* (1989–1990). He is president of the board of the New Israel Fund, the board chair for the National Center for Youth Law, and a board member for the Center for Community Change, the Public Welfare Foundation, the Center for Law and Social Policy, the Juvenile Law Center of Philadelphia, and many other organizations. His numerous awards include the Eason Monroe Courageous Advocate Award from the American Civil Liberties Union of Southern California (1996) and the Ned Pattison Award from the Capital Region chapter of the American Civil Liberties Union (1997). He graduated from Harvard Law School.

Harry J. Holzer is a professor and associate dean of Public Policy at Georgetown University, a visiting fellow at the Urban Institute, a research affiliate of the Institute for Research on Poverty at the University of Wisconsin–Madison, and a senior affiliate of the National Poverty Center at the University of Michigan. Formerly, he was chief economist for the U.S. Department of Labor and professor of economics at Michigan State University. He received both his A.B. and his Ph.D. in Economics from Harvard. Among his other books are *The Black Youth Employment Crisis* (coedited with Richard Freeman, University of Chicago Press, 1986); *What Employers Want: Job Prospects for Less-Educated Workers* (Russell Sage Foundation, 1996); *Employers and Welfare Recipients: The Effects of Welfare Reform in the Workplace* (with Michael Stoll, Public Policy Institute of California, 2001); and *Moving Up or Moving On: Who Advances in the Low-Wage Labor Market* (with Fredrik Andersson and Julia Lane, Russell Sage Foundation, 2005).

Paul Offner (1942–2004) enjoyed a distinguished career spanning government, research, and education. After earning his Ph.D. in economics from Princeton University, he was elected to the Wisconsin State Assembly, then to the Wisconsin State Senate. He served as deputy director of the Ohio Department of Human Services before moving to the federal government, first as a legislative assistant to Senator Daniel Patrick Moynihan, then as chief health and welfare counselor for the Senate Finance Committee. His accomplishments include terms as commissioner of Health Care Finance for the District of Columbia, as a research professor for Georgetown University's Institute for Health Care Research and Policy, and as a consultant for the Urban Institute. A prolific researcher and writer, he counted among his many publications *Medicaid and the States* (Century Foundation Press, 1999) and the *Journal of Human Resources* article "Labor Force Participation in the Ghetto" (1972).

Index

A

Academy for Educational Development
  Beacons Initiative evaluation, 44, 64n6
African-American men
  attitudes and behaviors, 24
  business cycle effect on employment, 16
  educational level and employment
    association, 15–16
  employment rates, 13, 18, 125
  idleness rates, 13–14, 123
  incarceration, 1, 24–26, 99, 108–109,
    120n16
  school enrollment and employment
    rates, 13, 16–19
  unpopularity with politicians, 31
After School Matters, 70, 127
  funding, 71
  limitations, 71
  outcomes data, 78n5
  programs, 70–71
after-school programs. *See* youth devel-
    opment efforts
Almeida, Cheryl, 53
alternative and charter high schools, 51
  community college programs and,
    53–54
  elements common to, 54

Henry Ford Academy, 52–53
  High Tech High School, 51–52
  relevance for youth, 74
Altschuler, David, 115
amnesty programs for child support
    payments, 104, 120n12, 130
Annie E. Casey Foundation, 8n1
  Jobs Initiative, 59
apprenticeship programs
  community colleges and, 54
  compared with STWOA, 62–63
  expanding, 49
  federal program recommendation, 62,
    127
  in Germany and Japan, 47
  Hillside Work-Scholarship Connection
    and, 44
  models for, 48
  private investment in, 49
  recommendation for, 60
ASM. *See* After School Matters
Aspen Institute, 58, 73

B

baby boomers
  retirement effect on the labor market,
    5, 27–28, 29, 30, 62, 123–124

Baby College, 69
Balanced Budget Act of 1997
    welfare-to-work grants, 105
Beacons Initiative, 40, 42–43, 44
    evaluation of, 44, 64n6
    funding, 42
    national sites, 43
    school-based community center
        example, 74
    use of school buildings after school, 40
Besharov, Douglas J., 29
Big Brothers Big Sisters
    evaluation of, 44, 60, 64n3, 126
    focus on at-risk youth, 40
Bill and Melinda Gates Foundation, 52
BLS. See Bureau of Labor Statistics
Boston Gun Project, 117, 118
    Operation Ceasefire, 118
Boys and Girls Clubs
    focus on at-risk youth, 40
Brand, Betsy, 47
Bureau of Labor Statistics
    growth of jobs not requiring college
        degrees, 29–30
    occupational growth, 29
    teen employment rate, 1, 9n2
Bush administration
    prisoner reentry initiative, 118–119
    school reform efforts, 45

C
Campaign for Youth, 61
Canada
    Self-Sufficiency Project, 82–83
Canada, Geoffrey, 41–42, 68–69, 75
Card, David, 86
Career Academies, 49, 126
    compared with career and technical
        education, 49–50
    evaluation of, 61, 66n28
    positive impact on employment and
        earnings, 51
    relevance for youth, 74
    success of, 50
    tracking out of college curricula and, 46
career and technical education, 45–46
    compared with Career Academies,
        49–50

criticism of, 46
decline in enrollment, 45
funding, 46, 47
reform of, 46–47
tracking out of college and, 46
Carl D. Perkins Vocational and Technical
    Education Act, 46, 47
CASES. See Center for Alternative Sen-
    tencing and Employment Strategies
Center for Alternative Sentencing and
    Employment Strategies, 114–115
Center for Employment Opportunities,
    59, 66n25, 114, 116, 117
    Neighborhood Work Project, 116
    Vocational Development Program, 116
Center for Employment Training, 58–59,
    126
    evaluation of, 58–59, 65n23
    sites, 58
Center for Governmental Research
    Hillside Work-Scholarship Connection
        evaluation, 44
CEO. See Center for Employment
    Opportunities
CET. See Center for Employment Training
CGR. See Center for Governmental
    Research
Challenge Grants, 77
Chapin Hall Center for Children
    Beacons Initiative evaluation, 44, 64n6
charter high schools. See alternative and
    charter high schools
child support. See also noncustodial
    parents
    amnesty programs, 104, 120n12, 130
    arrears in, 103, 104, 120n12, 129
    earned income tax credit and, 90–91,
        93n17, 129
    employment and, 25–26, 32, 36n30,
        36n31, 129–130
    ex-offenders and, 32, 112
    garnishment of wages and, 103, 129
    paid as percentage of gross income, 100
    passing through to custodial parents,
        36n32, 100, 102–103, 107, 130
    unrealistic amounts, 100, 101,
        103–104, 107, 129

work incentives for noncustodial
parents, 100–101, 129–130
child support orders
default orders, 103–104, 107, 129
policy recommendations, 101–102,
103–104, 107, 130
reviewing, 104, 107, 119n4
work incentives and, 100–101, 129, 130
childless individuals
earned income tax credit and, 7, 9n6,
88–89, 93n13, 93n14, 94–97, 129
citywide government systems, 68, 70–71,
74, 127
cognitive skills
employment association, 20–22, 31, 32,
125
Cohen, Marie, 29
community colleges
College Bound program, 53
Excel Program, 53–54
financial aid, 54
high school programs combined with,
53
remedial education and training, 54–55
Community Prep High School, 114–115
Community Pride, 69
community systems
accessibility, 76–77
citywide government systems, 68,
70–71, 74, 127
forming systems, 74–76
formula grants for, 77–78
funding, 71–73, 75, 76, 77–78, 127
need for, 3–4, 7, 32, 67, 127
neighborhood-based, 68–69, 74–76
neighborhood effects and, 67–68
policy recommendations, 76–78
computer technicians, 29
Cooperative Home Care Associates, 66n24
craft occupations, 29
criminal activity. See also ex-offenders;
incarceration
employment and, 24–26, 32
CTE. See career and technical education

D
Daly, Maggie, 70–71
Daschle, Sen. Tom

earned income tax credit proposal,
93n15
default child support orders, 103–104,
107, 129
DeVry University, 71
Disability Insurance, 92n2
disconnection, 1, 8n1, 13–14, 26–27, 123
costs, 26–27
economic prospects and, 2, 26–27
high-poverty neighborhoods and, 3,
19, 35n25, 67–68
men compared with women, 1–2
personal choices and, 2, 3, 23
discrimination
employment and, 3, 23, 31, 35n23
The Door
focus on at-risk youth, 40
dropouts
alternative and charter high schools
and, 6, 53
career and technical education and, 46
educational level effect on wages, 18,
80–81
employment rates and, 18, 20, 38, 81
incarceration and, 34n10
measurement of rates, 33n5
rate among minorities, 34n10, 38, 45,
64n1

E
Early College High School program, 53, 55
earned income tax credit
child support payments and, 90–91
childless individuals and, 7, 9n6, 32,
84, 88–89, 93n14, 94–97, 129
cost of, 84, 92n5
custodial parents and, 7, 26, 88–89, 90
effect on work, 84, 93n19
expanding, 7, 87
impact on employment rates, 82, 87–88
for low-income workers, 7, 79, 87, 91,
126, 128
marriage penalty, 88–90, 91, 94–97, 129
working mothers and, 7, 19, 83, 84, 124
noncustodial parents and, 7, 32, 90–91,
94–97, 128
Earth Tech, 70

Economic Policy Institute
    minimum wage benefit, 85
education and training. See also alterna-
    tive and charter high schools; Career
    Academies; career and technical
    education; school enrollment;
    school-to-work programs
    community colleges, 5, 6, 32, 39, 53,
        54–55, 72, 126, 128
    evaluation of, 63–64
    ex-offenders, 110, 112–113, 120n20
    funding, 131–132
    national apprenticeship program,
        62–63, 127, 128
    policy recommendations, 6–7, 60–64,
        126–128
    second-chance training programs, 5,
        56–60
    youth development, 5, 40–44, 126
EITC. See earned income tax credit
elastic labor supply, 82, 85, 120n5
employment. See also idleness; minimum
    wage
    child support enforcement and, 25–26,
        32, 36n30
    decline in real wages, 20
    demand for college-educated workers,
        28, 29–30
    discrimination and, 3, 23, 26, 31, 35n23
    dropouts and, 18, 20, 38, 81
    early work experience, 5, 22, 24, 26, 30,
        37, 125
    ex-offenders, 25–26, 32, 109–110,
        120n18
    growth of jobs not requiring college
        degrees, 28–30, 36n39, 38
    incarceration and, 24–26
    informal networks and, 23, 31
    labor supply and, 26, 28, 34n13, 82,
        83–86, 90, 92n3, 120n5
    less-educated men and women and, 7,
        15–16, 19–26, 123
    noncustodial parents, 25, 32, 101,
        105–106, 107–108
    popular culture and, 23–24
    school enrollment and, 12–13, 16–19,
        124

skills mismatch and, 21
spatial mismatch and, 19, 22, 23, 26,
    31, 35n21, 125
Supported Work program, 111, 117,
    120n19
teens and, 1, 9n2
test scores and, 20–22, 37, 38, 125
welfare policies and, 19, 31, 34n11
Employment and Technology Center, 42,
    44
Empowerment Zones
    Youth Opportunity sites, 72
Enterprise Communities
    Youth Opportunity sites, 72
ETC. See Employment and Technology
    Center
ex-offenders. See also incarceration
    background checks and, 110, 120n17
    challenges, 110
    characteristics and behaviors, 111
    child support obligations, 112
    education and training programs, 110,
        112–113, 120n19
    employment and, 25–26, 32, 109–110,
        120n18, 125–126
    family relationships and, 110–111
    Federal Prison Industries and, 113,
        121n23
    policy recommendations, 119, 130–131
    postrelease services and supports,
        114–117
    prerelease planning, 111, 113–114
    prisoner reentry initiative, 118–119
    recidivism rates among young
        offenders, 111
    Safety First project, 117
    stigma associated with criminal record,
        110
    Supported Work program and, 111,
        117, 120n19
    tracking after release, 112
    transitional jobs programs, 117
Excel Program, 53–54

F
Family Support Act of 1988, 105
Family Support Center, 69

Federal Prison Industries, 113, 121n22,
    121n23
financial incentives for low-wage work
    Disability Insurance and, 92n2
    earned income tax credit and, 7, 19, 32,
        79, 82, 84, 90
    Edmund Phelps proposal, 87, 93n10
    elastic labor supply and, 82, 85, 120n5
    lower wages and reduced employment,
        82
    minimum wage, 84–87
    minimum wage compared with wage
        subsidies and tax credits, 83–84
    New Hope Project, 83, 90
    policy options, 83–84, 87–92, 128–129
    underground employment and, 82
    wage subsidies and tax credits, 87–92
Florida Department of Corrections
    Office of Citizens' Services, 113
Focus Hope program, 59
Ford Motor Company, 52
formula grants, 77–78
4-H clubs, 40
FPI. See Federal Prison Industries
Frank, Rep. Barney
    Federal Prison Industries restrictions,
        121n23
Freeman, Richard B., 108–109, 121n24
Friends of the Island Academy, 114, 115

G
Gallery37 program, 70
Greenfield Village, 52
Grogger, Jeffrey, 82

H
Harlem Children's Zone, 41–42, 68, 127
    Baby College, 69
    Community Pride, 69
    Employment and Technology Center,
        42, 44
    evaluation of, 126
    expansion of, 69
    Family Support Center, 69
    funding, 74
    Harlem Gems, 69
    Harlem Peacemakers, 69

    success of, 69
    10-year growth plan, 69
    TRUCE program, 42, 44
Harlem Gems, 69
The Harlem Overheard, 42
Harlem Peacemakers, 69
HCZ. See Harlem Children's Zone
health occupations, 29
Henry Ford Academy
    curriculum, 52
    demographics, 52
Henry Ford Museum, 52
HFA. See Henry Ford Academy
high school education and training efforts
    alternative and charter schools, 51–54
    Career Academies, 49–51
    career and technical education, 45–47
    focus of, 5
    school reform efforts, 45
    school-to-work programs, 47–49
High Tech High School, 51–52
    funding, 52
Higher Education Act, 46, 61
Hillside Work-Scholarship Connection, 43
    apprenticeships, 44
    career planning and placement
        curriculum, 43–44
    evaluation of, 44
    Individualized Development Plan, 43
Hispanic men. See also Mexican men;
        Puerto Rican men
    dropout rates, 38
    educational level and employment,
        15–16
    employment rates, 13, 18–19, 38
    idleness rates, 13–14
    incarceration, 99, 108
    lower wage jobs and, 35n22
    school enrollment and employment
        rates, 13, 16–19
Holzer, Harry J., 16, 25–26, 101, 109
HW-SC. See Hillside Work-Scholarship
    Connection

I
IAP. See Intensive Aftercare Program
idleness, 1–2, 9n3. See also employment

idleness (*continued*)
   educational attainment and associated
      labor market outcomes, 17–19
   factors, 19–26
   rates, 12–14
   school enrollment and employment
      rates and, 12–17
incarceration. *See also* ex-offenders
   African-American men, 1, 24–26, 99,
      108–109, 120n16
   costs to families and children, 27
   dropouts and, 34n10
   Hispanic men, 99, 108
   length of, 108
   negative impacts on young men, 109
   public safety costs and, 26–27
   rising rates and reduced labor force par-
      ticipation among black men, 25–26
   white men, 99
industrial jobs, 20
informal networks, 23, 31
   Intensive Aftercare Program, 114, 115
   ISUS Trade and Technology Prep, 53
Intensive Aftercare Program, 114, 115

J
Job Corps, 56, 126
   community-based system model, 5, 74
   evaluation of, 57, 61, 117
   ex-offenders and, 117
   funding, 61
Job Start, 57
Job Training Partnership Act, 57
Jobs-Plus program, 73, 78n7
John V. Lindsay Wildcat Charter School,
   114, 115
   Wildcat Service Corporation, 116
JTPA. *See* Job Training Partnership Act
Juhn, Chinhui, 81, 82

K
Katz, Lawrence F., 82
Katzmann, Gary S., 117
Kennedy, Sen. Edward
   minimum wage proposal, 86

Kennedy School of Government
   Operation Ceasefire evaluation, 118
Krueger, Alan G., 86

L
La Bodega de la Familia, 113–114
LaGuardia Community College
   Excel Program, 53–54
LEHD program. *See* Longitudinal
   Employer Household Dynamics
   program
Lerman, Robert I., 48
Longitudinal Employer Household
   Dynamics program, 66n29

M
Manpower Demonstration Research
   Corporation
   Career Academies study, 49, 50
   Jobs-Plus evaluation, 73, 78n4
   Opening Doors project, 55
   Parents' Fair Share evaluation, 105–106
marriage penalty
   earned income tax credit and, 88–90,
      91, 94–97, 129
   reducing, 89–90
Mathematica Policy Research, Inc., 64n4
MDRC. *See* Manpower Demonstration
   Research Corporation
Medicaid, 9n5
   custodial parents and, 26
Medicare
   baby boomers and, 30
Mexican men
   employment rates, 17
Middle College High School program, 53
Miller, Rep. George
   minimum wage proposal, 86
minimum wage
   benefit to workers in lower-income
      families, 85
   compared with wage subsidies and tax
      credits, 83–84
   employers' investment in training
      young workers and, 92n8

erosion in the value of, 85
historical background, 84–85
inflation and, 84
labor market supply and demand and, 85
production worker wage and, 86
proposals for, 86–87
raising, 7, 32, 85–87, 128
reduction in the demand for youth labor, 83, 85
state-set, 84
tight labor market effect, 86
transitional jobs programs and, 117
youth employment and, 86
mismatch. *See* spatial mismatch
Moving to Opportunity program, 35n21
MTO program. *See* Moving to Opportunity program
Murphy, Kevin, 82

N
National Assessment of Vocational Education, 46
National Council on Crime and Delinquency
Intensive Aftercare Program evaluation, 114
National Educational Longitudinal Survey
test scores and association with employment, 20–21, 37, 38, 125
National Governors Association
school reform, 45
National Youth Employment Coalition, 61
nationally funded community systems, 71–73
NCLB. *See* No Child Left Behind Act
neighborhood-based nonprofit systems, 68–69
Neighborhood Work Project, 116
NELS. *See* National Educational Longitudinal Survey
New Hope Project, 83, 90, 128
No Child Left Behind Act, 37, 76, 112
noncustodial parents. *See also* child support

arrears in child support, 103–104, 129
child support orders, 100–102, 107, 129
default child support orders, 103–104, 107, 129
disposable income, 101
earned income tax credit and, 90–91, 128
employment and, 25, 32, 101, 105–106, 107–108, 125–126
food stamp availability, 119n3
helping low-wage noncustodial parents with child support, 101–102
improving the earnings of, 105–106, 107–108
marginal tax rates and, 101, 108
passing through child support, 102–103, 107, 130
percentage of gross income dedicated to child support, 100
policy recommendations, 107–112
stipends with job training for, 106
taxes on the earnings of, 26, 36n32
work incentives for, 100–101
North Carolina Vocational Delivery System, 113

O
OATELS. *See* Office of Apprenticeship, Training, Employer, and Labor Services
Office of Apprenticeship, Training, Employer, and Labor Services, 62
Offner, Paul, 16, 25–26
offshoring, 36n34
Omega Boys Club
focus on at-risk youth, 40
Opening Doors project, 55
Operation Ceasefire, 118

P
Parents' Fair Share initiative, 105
evaluation of, 105–106, 107–108
Pell Grants, 54, 55, 61, 127
Perkins Act. *See* Carl D. Perkins Vocational and Technical Education Act

PFS. *See* Parents' Fair Share initiative
Phelps, Edmund, 87, 93n10
Philliber Research Associates, 44
popular culture
    employment and, 23–24
Portland Community College
    College Bound program, 53
Primus, Wendell, 106
Puerto Rican men
    employment rates, 17

Q
Quantum Opportunities Program, 40, 126
    evaluation of, 44, 60–61, 64n3
QUEST program, 59

R
Raphael, Steven, 109
Reagan, Pres. Ronald
    support for earned income tax credit,
        93n12
The Real Deal, 42
remedial education
    community colleges and, 54, 55
    second-chance training programs,
        56–60
The Renaissance University for Commu-
    nity Education. *See* TRUCE program

S
Safer Foundation, 114, 116–117
Safety First project, 117
SCHIP. *See* State Children's Health
    Insurance Program
school enrollment, 13, 16–19. *See also*
    dropouts; education and training
    access to community colleges, 32
    business cycle and, 16
    educational level effect on wages, 80–81
    employment rates and, 12–13
    gender gap, 13, 22
    growth of jobs not requiring college
        degrees, 29–30, 36n39
    less-educated men and women and, 7,
        15–16, 19–26
    work during the school year and
        wages, 36n40

school reform, 45, 47, 116
School-to-Work Opportunities Act
    apprenticeship programs and, 62
    expiration of, 48
    provisions, 48
    state activities, 49
    tracking out of college curricula and, 48
school-to-work programs. *See also*
    apprenticeship programs
    assumptions about, 47
    employers' willingness to invest in, 6,
        47–48, 65n13
    School-to-Work Opportunities Act
        and, 48–49
second-chance training programs
    Center for Employment Training,
        58–59
    community organizations and, 59
    cost-effectiveness of, 57–58
    Focus Hope, 59
    funding, 55, 58
    Job Corps, 55, 56, 58
    National Guard Youth ChalleNGe
        Program, 56
    QUEST, 59
    sectoral programs, 39, 56, 58–59, 65n22
    success of, 59
    WIRENet, 59
    Wisconsin Regional Training Partner-
        ship, 59
    Youth Conservation Corps, 55, 57
    Youth Service Corps, 55, 57, 58
        YouthBuild, 56–57
Self-Sufficiency Project, 82–83
    cost, 90
Sensenbrenner, Rep. Jim
    Federal Prison Industries restrictions,
        121n23
Sinclair Community College
    ISUS Trade and Technology Prep, 53
Social Security
    baby boomers and, 30
Sorensen, Elaine, 25–26, 93n18
spatial mismatch
    employment and, 19, 22, 23, 26, 31,
        35n21, 125

Sports37 program, 70–71
SSP. *See* Self-Sufficiency Project
State Children's Health Insurance
    Program, 9n5
Steinberg, Adria, 53
STEP. *See* Summer Training and
    Employment Program
Stoll, Michael, 109
STWOA. *See* School-to-Work Opportuni-
    ties Act
Sum, Andrew, 16
Summer Training and Employment
    Program, 57
Supported Work program, 111, 117,
    120n19

T
Talent Development High Schools, 50
    evaluation of, 50–51, 64n9
TANF. *See* Temporary Assistance for
    Needy Families
tax credits. *See also* earned income tax
    credit
    compared with minimum wage and
        wage subsidies, 83–84
    refundable, 84
Tech Prep program, 53
Tech37 program, 70
Temporary Assistance for Needy Families
    community system funding, 76
    education and training funding, 54, 55,
        61
    noncustodial parents and, 105, 106, 107
Ten Point Coalition, 117, 118
test scores
    association with employment, 20–21,
        37, 38, 125
Topel, Robert, 82
training programs. *See* education and
    training
transitional jobs programs, 117
TRUCE program, 42, 44
21st Century Community Learning
    Centers, 41
    evaluation of, 64n4, 66n28
    funding, 76

U
Uggen, Christopher, 111
underground employment, 14, 25, 33n3,
    82, 103, 120n18
U.S. Department of Commerce
    apprenticeship programs and, 62
U.S. Department of Education
    education and training programs
        evaluation, 63
    National Assessment of Vocational
        Education, 46
U.S. Department of Health and Human
    Services
    education and training programs
        evaluation, 63
U.S. Department of Labor. *See also* Youth
    Opportunity
    apprenticeship programs and, 62
    education and training programs
        evaluation of, 63, 128
    Office of Apprenticeship, Training,
        Employer, and Labor Services, 62
    Youth Offender Demonstration Project,
        114

V
Vera Institute of Justice, 114
Vocational Development Program, 116
vocational education. *See* career and
    technical education

W
wage subsidies
    administrative challenges, 93n11
    compared with minimum wage and
        tax credits, 83–84
    cost of, 87
    proposal for, 87
Wegmans Food Markets, 43–44
Weisberg, Lois, 70
welfare policies
    effects on employment, 19, 31, 34n11
welfare reform, 4, 34n11, 103, 123
Welfare-to-Work grants, 58, 105
Westat, Inc., 73
white men
    employment rates, 13

white men (*continued*)
  idleness rates, 13, 14
  incarceration, 99
WIA. *See* Workforce Investment Act
Wildcat Academy. *See* John V. Lindsay
    Wildcat Charter School
Wildcat Service Corporation, 116
Wilson, William Julius, 20, 67–68
WIRENet program, 59
Wisconsin
  passing through child support, 103
  Regional Training Partnership, 59
women
  disconnection and, 1–2, 14
  educational level and employment, 15,
    81
  employment, 4, 12–13, 15, 16–17, 18,
    19, 34n11, 81, 92n1, 123, 124
  as heads of households, 24, 35n25
  idleness and, 14, 125
  idleness rates, 13, 14, 123, 124
    school enrollment, 4, 12–13, 18
Words37 program, 71
Workforce Investment Act, 46, 55, 76
Workforce Investment Boards, 54, 55, 61,
    72, 76

Y
YO. *See* Youth Opportunity
Youth Conservation Corps, 57
  community-based system model, 74
Youth Councils, 76

youth development efforts
  Beacons Initiative, 40, 42, 43, 44
  evaluation of, 44
  Harlem Children's Zone, 41–42, 43, 44
  Hillside Work-Scholarship Connection,
    43–44
  historical background, 40–41
  principles, 41
  success of, 69
  White House report on, 67
Youth Fair Chance, 71
Youth Offender Demonstration Project,
    114
Youth Opportunities Unlimited, 71
Youth Opportunity, 71–72, 127
  evaluation, 73
  funding, 72, 78n6
  practical knowledge from, 77
  programs and services, 72
  state juvenile justice systems and, 73
Youth Service Corps, 57, 126
  community-based system model, 5, 74
  evaluation of, 61, 117
  ex-offenders and, 117
  impact of, 57
YouthBuild, 56
  community-based system model, 5, 74
  evaluation of, 61, 126
  funding, 61
  ISUS Trade and Technology Prep and,
    53
  sites, 56
  "YouthBuild way," 57